Easy Christian Coloring Book
for Adults

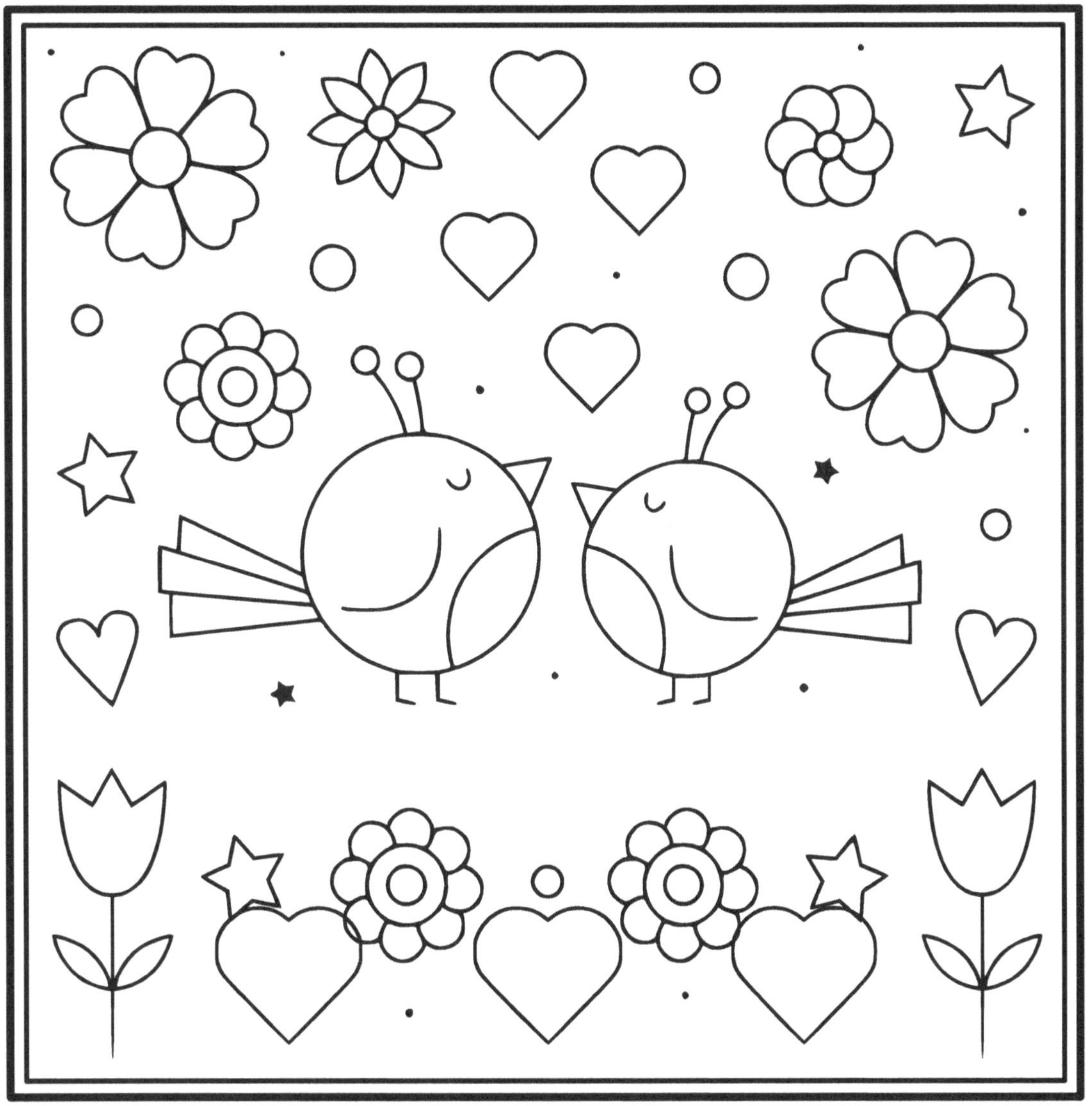

Featuring Large-Print Bible Psalms

Copyright Spring Lane Press

Tips for Coloring:

We hope you find time to enjoy this coloring book. It is our goal to engage your mind and encourage you to relax at the same time.

1) Find a quiet place free of distractions.

2) Cut out or tear out the coloring sheet if you wish.

3) Use coloring pencils or markers to color. Each coloring page is blank on the opposite side to allow for color bleed-through.

4) Let your mind wander and relax as you color.

5) Don't worry about being perfect!

6) Read and reflect on the Bible Psalm which accompanies each picture. Be comforted and reassured by the words of the Lord.

7) Enjoy and have a blessed day!

For your loyal love extends beyond the sky, and your faithfulness reaches the clouds.

— Psalm 57:10 (NET)

Certainly, O Lord, you are kind and forgiving, and show great faithfulness to all who cry out to you.

— Psalm 86:5 (NET)

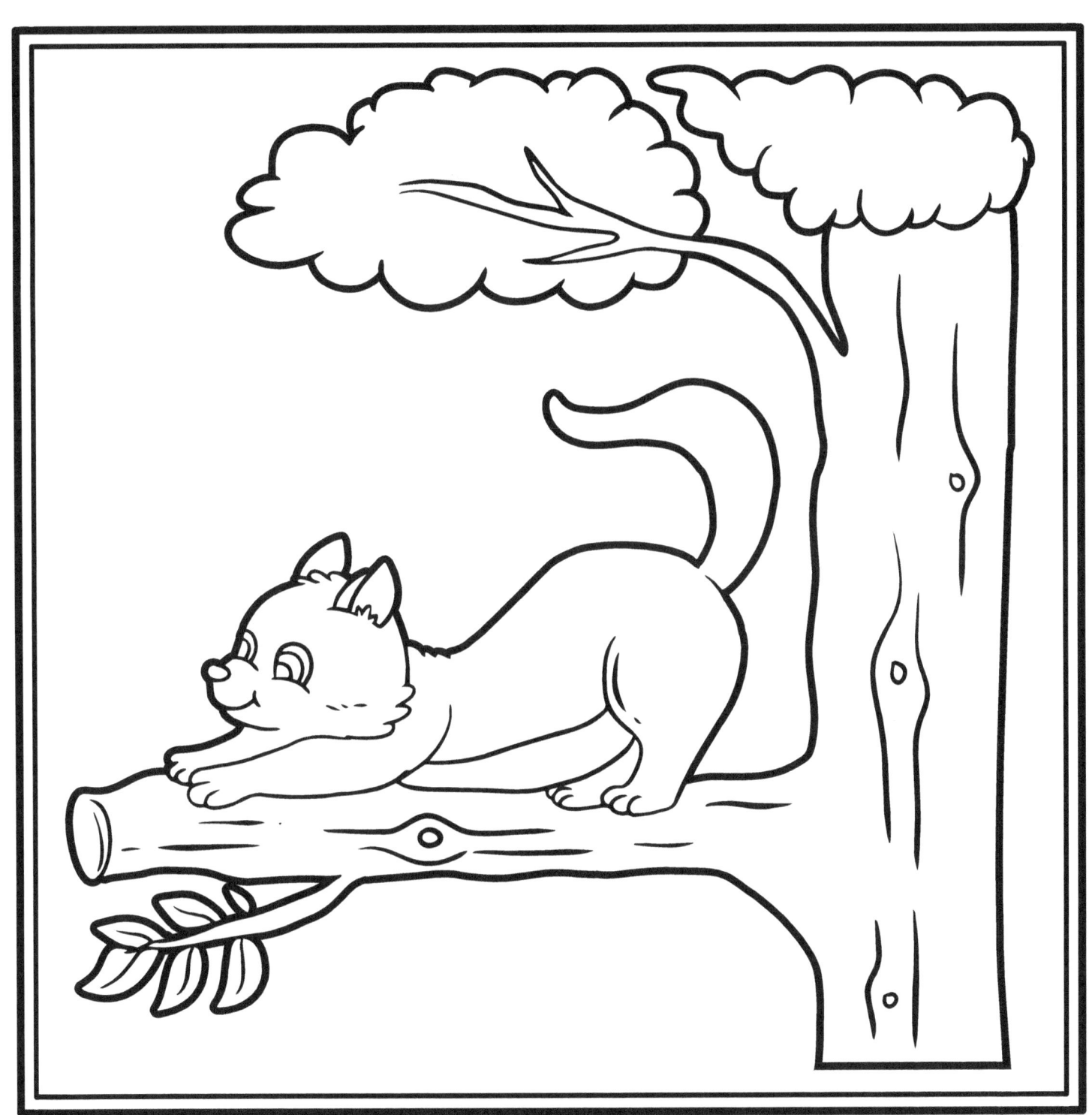

But you, Lord, are a shield that protects me;
you are my glory and the one who restores me.

— Psalm 3:3 (NET)

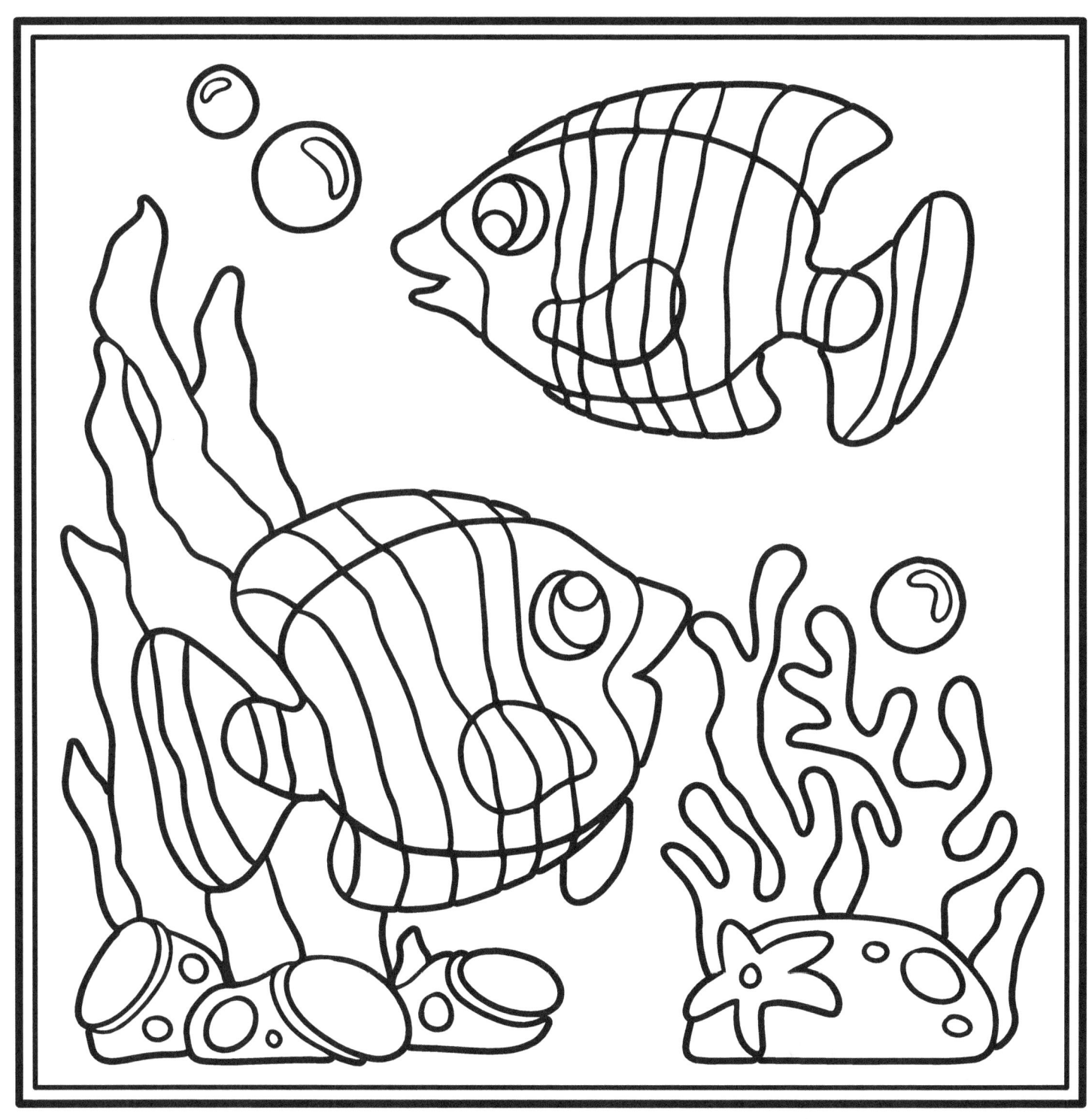

This is the day which the Lord hath made; we will rejoice and be glad in it.

— Psalm 118:24 (KJV)

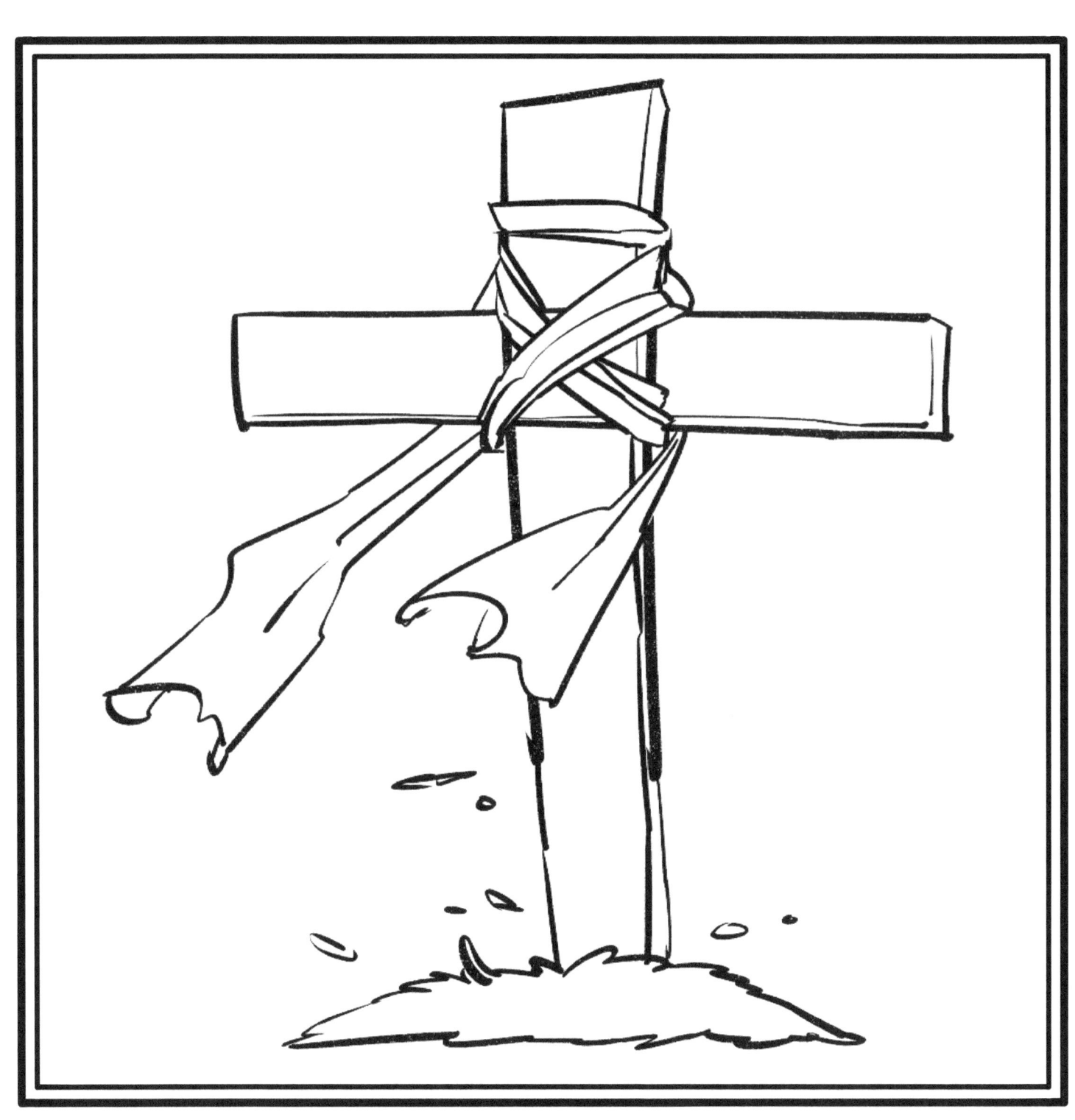

God be merciful unto us, and bless us; and cause his face to shine upon us.

— Psalm 67:1 (KJV)

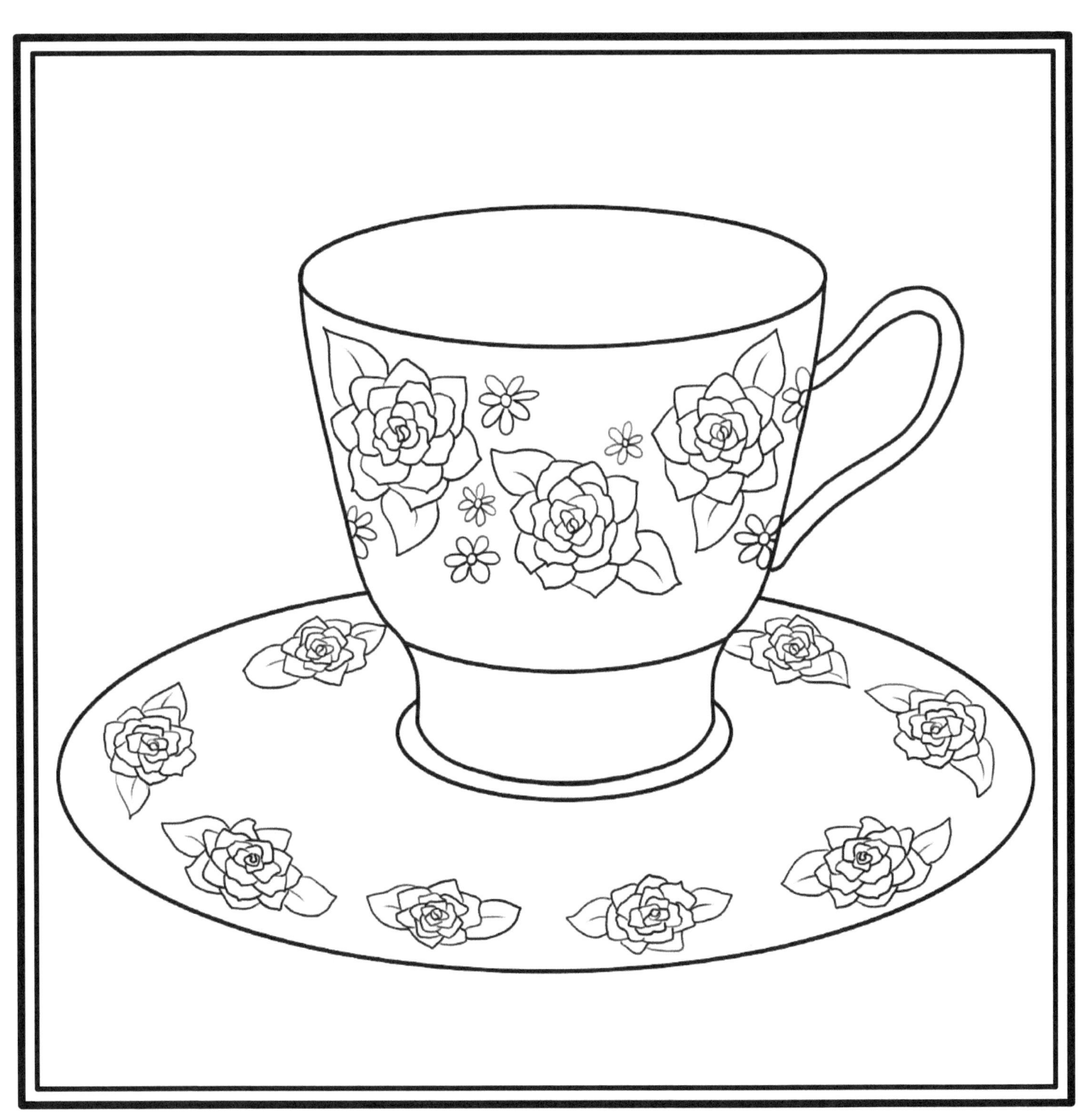

I constantly trust in the Lord; because he is at my right hand, I will not be shaken.

— Psalm 16:8 (NET)

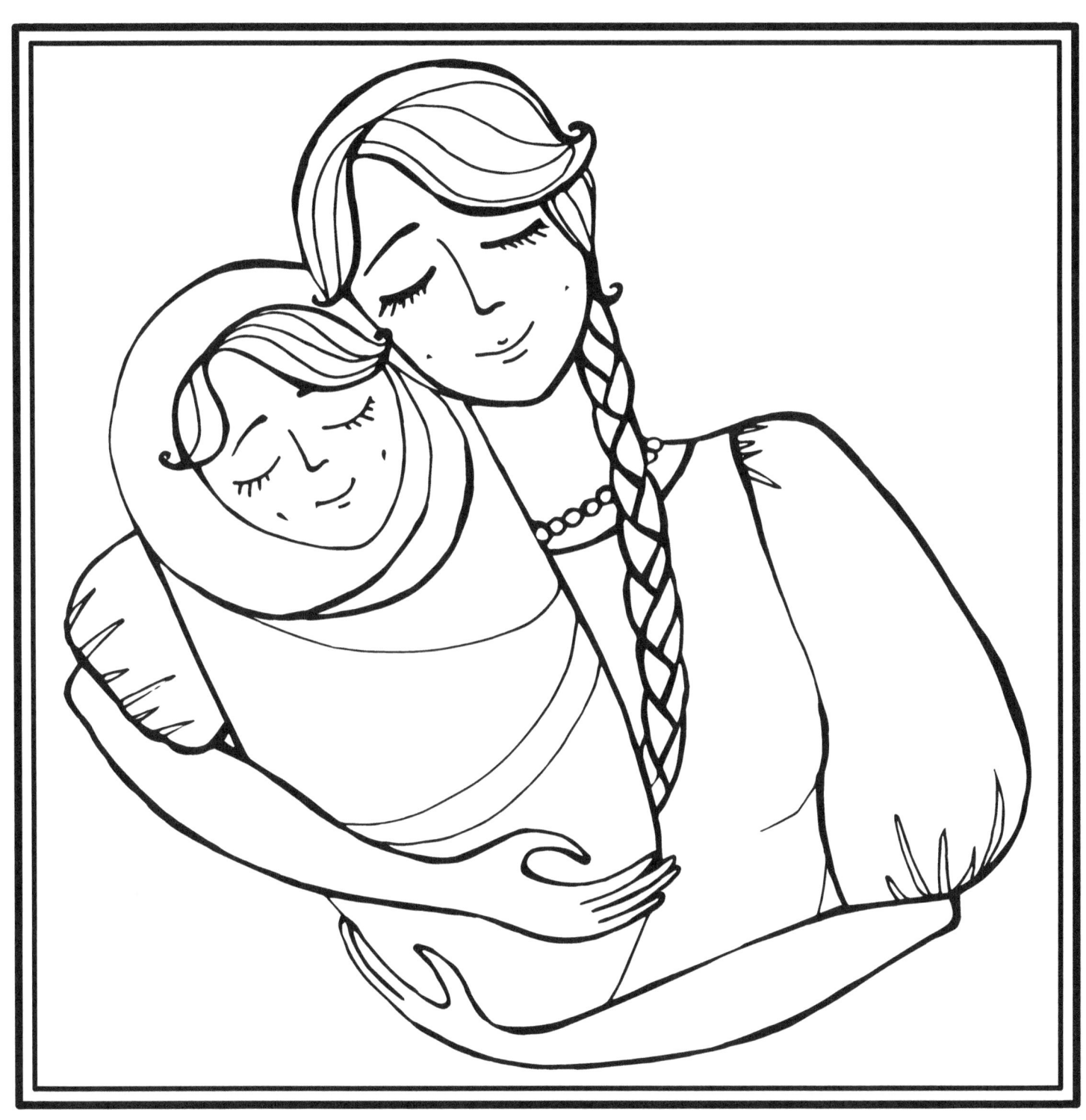

I will say of the Lord, He is my refuge and my fortress: my God; in him will I trust.

— Psalm 91:2 (KJV)

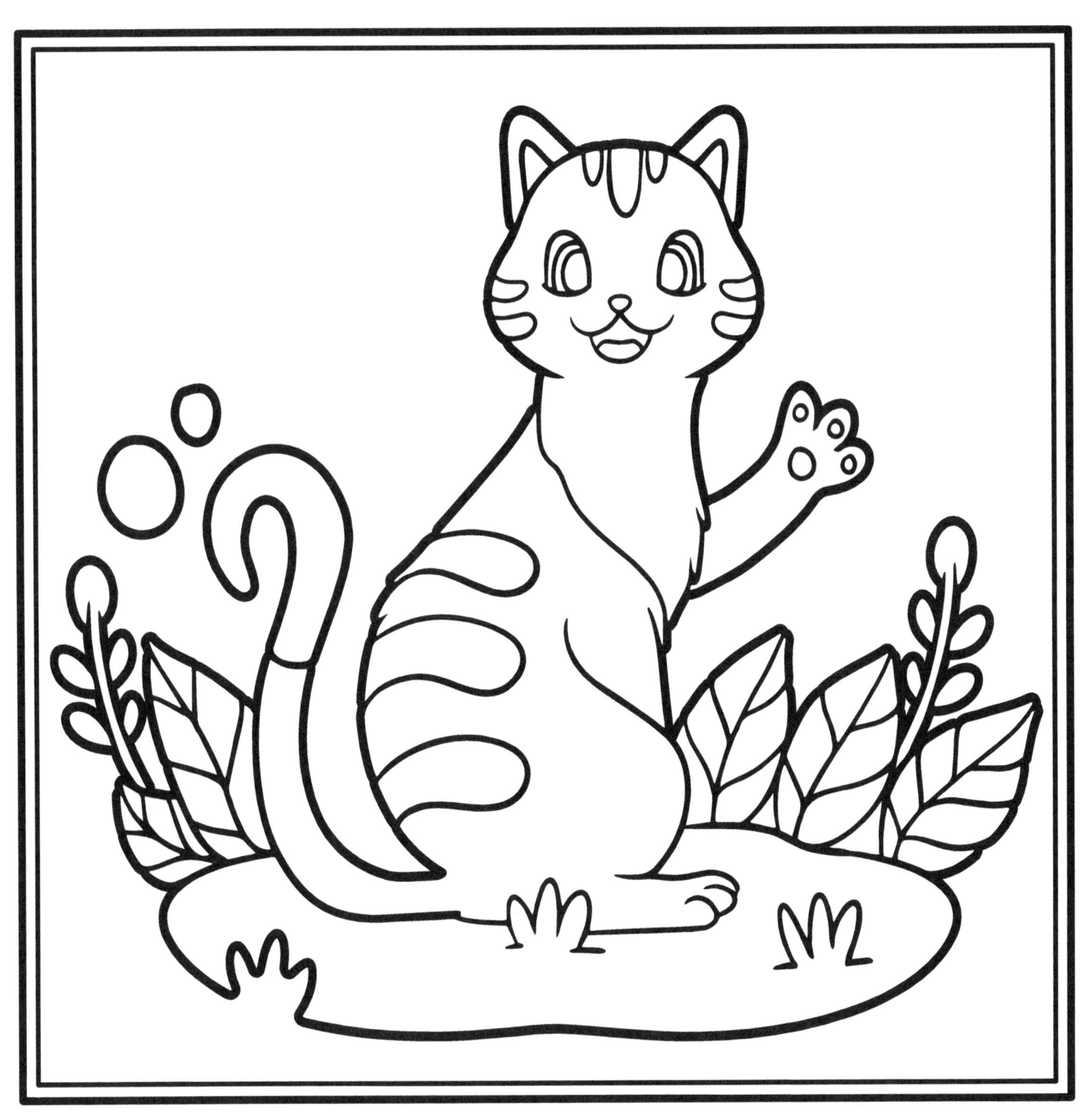

The Lord is my strength and song,
and is become my salvation.
— Psalm 118:14 (KJV)

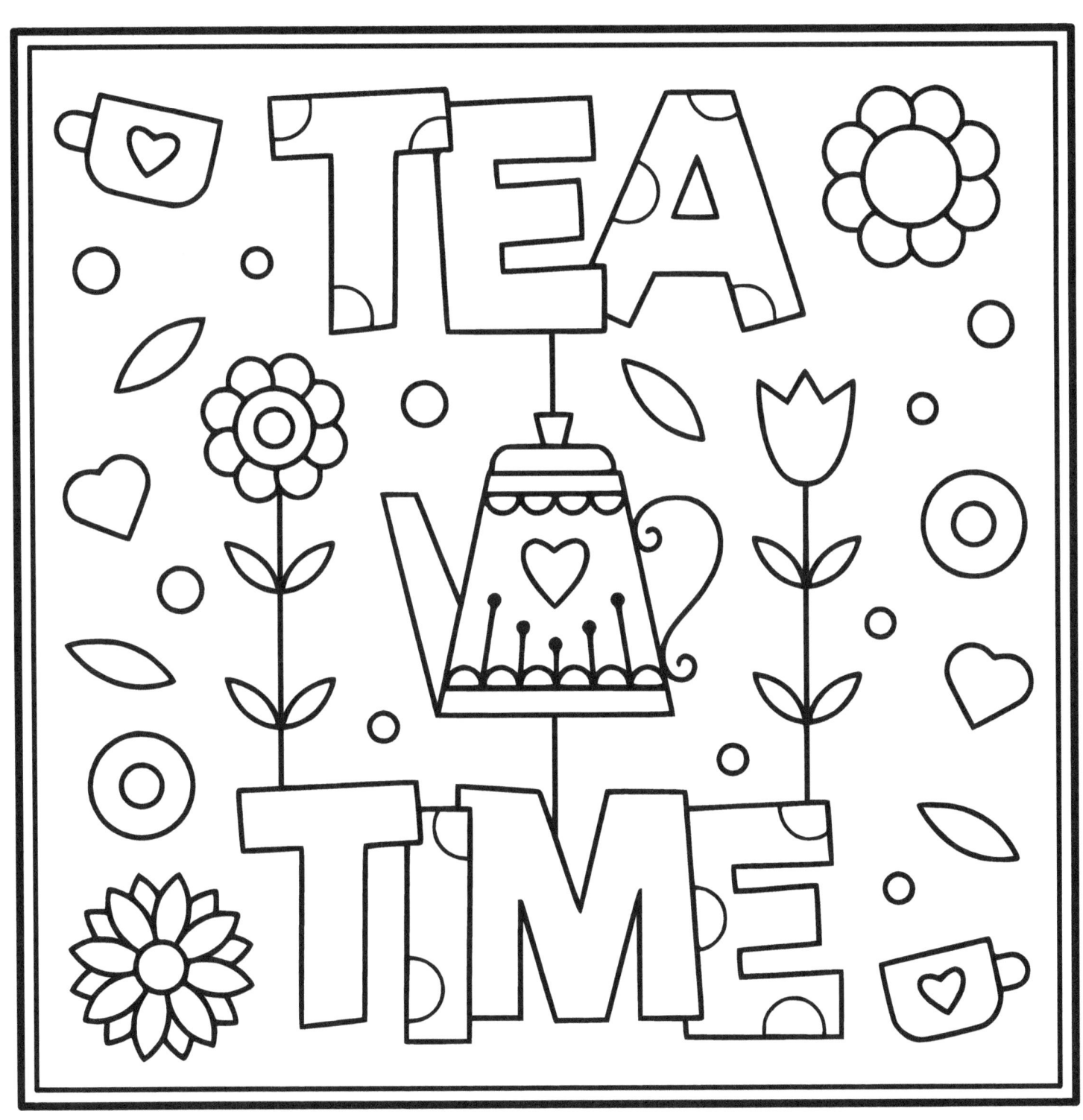

I will lift up mine eyes unto the hills, from whence cometh my help. My help cometh from the Lord, which made heaven and earth.

— Psalm 121:1-2 (KJV)

The Lord is my light and my salvation; whom shall I fear? the Lord is the strength of my life; of whom shall I be afraid?

— Psalm 27:1 (KJV)

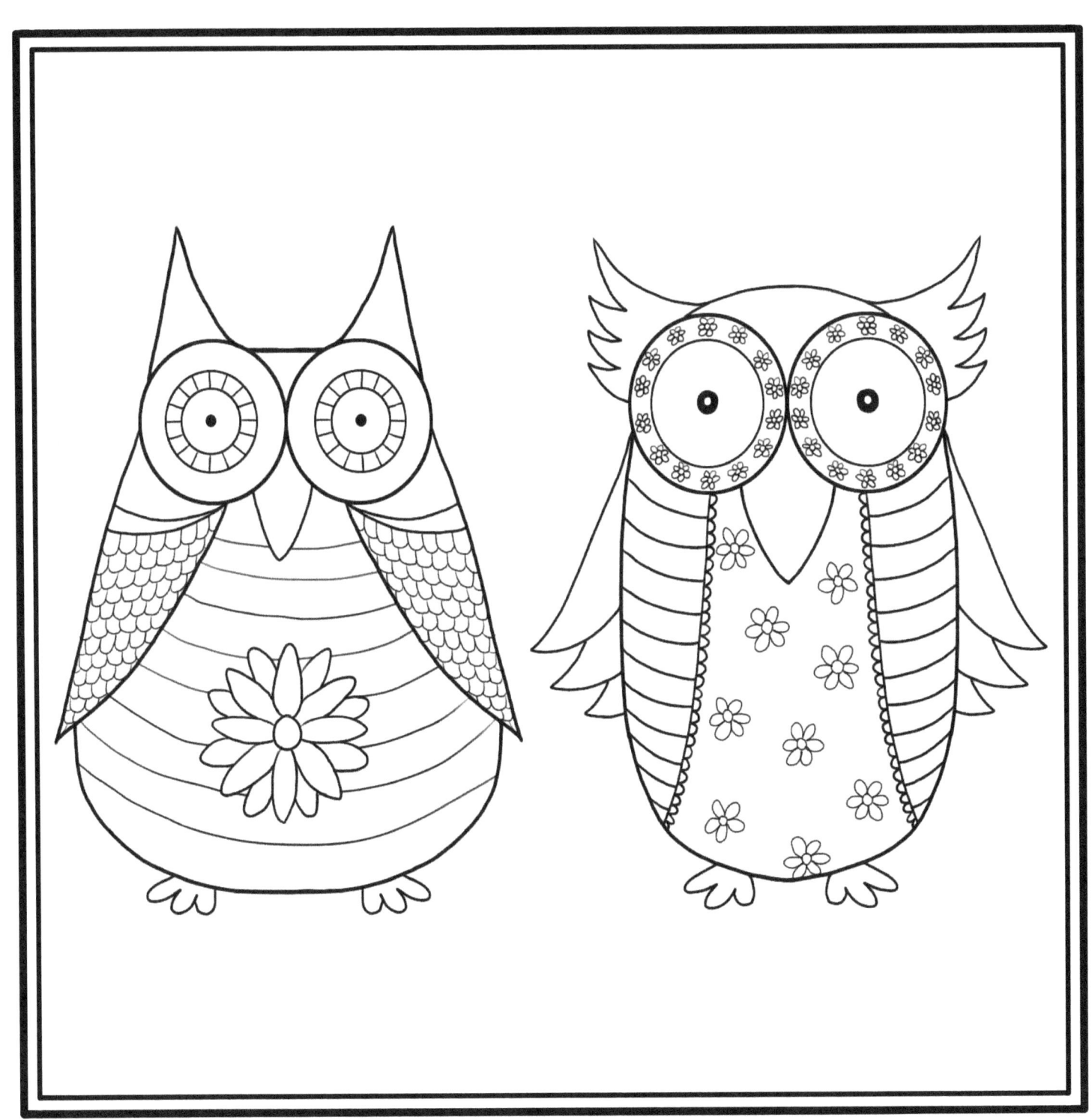

The heavens declare the glory of God;
the sky displays his handiwork.

— Psalm 19:1 (NET)

The Lord is my shepherd; I shall not want.
He maketh me to lie down in green pastures:
he leadeth me beside the still waters.

— Psalm 23:1-2 (KJV)

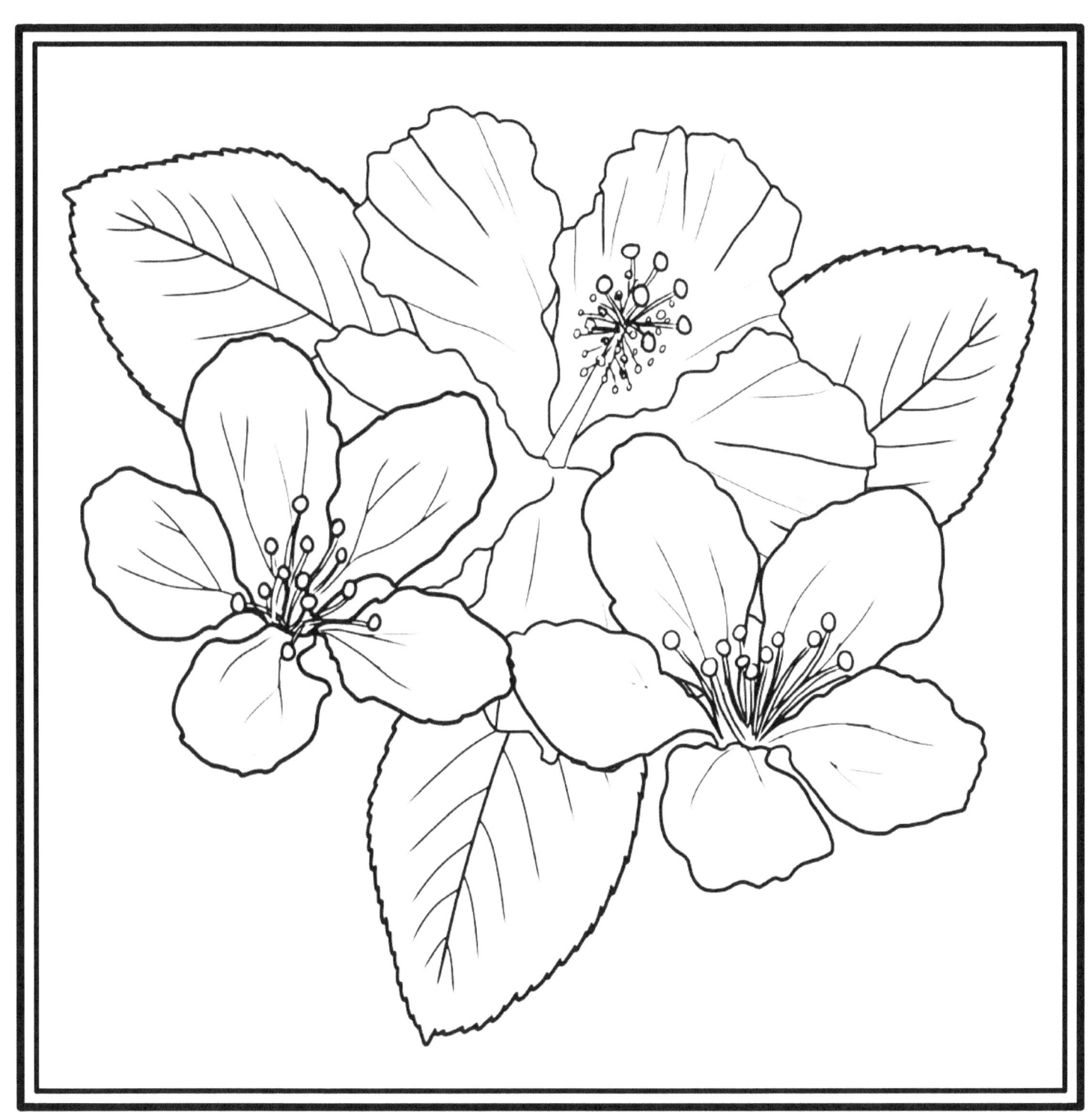

The Lord also will be a refuge for the oppressed, a refuge in times of trouble.

— Psalm 9:9 (KJV)

Throw your burden upon the Lord,
and he will sustain you.

— Psalm 55:22 (NET)

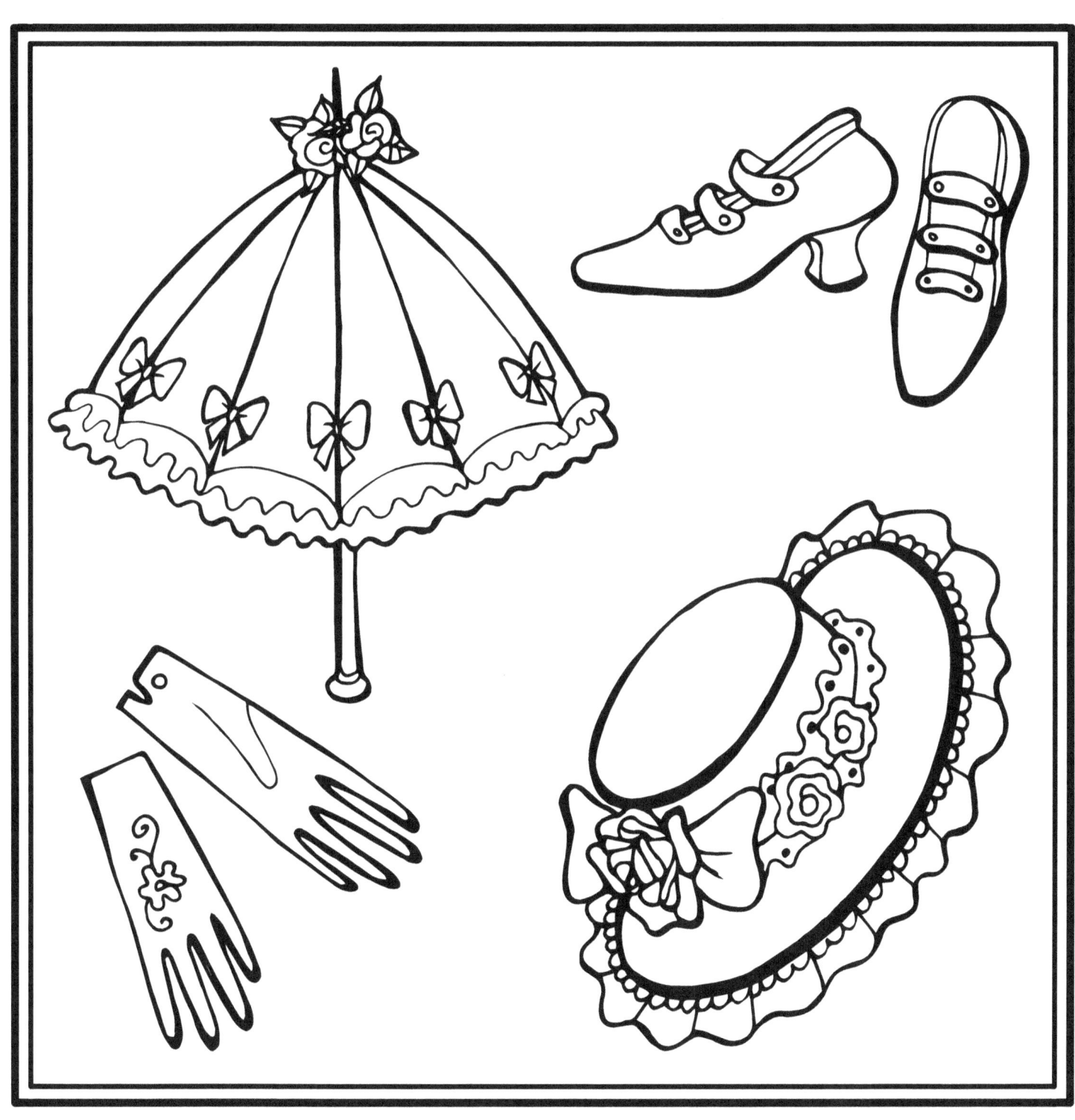

Acknowledge that the Lord is God.
He made us and we belong to him,
we are his people, the sheep of his pasture.

— Psalm 100:3 (NET)

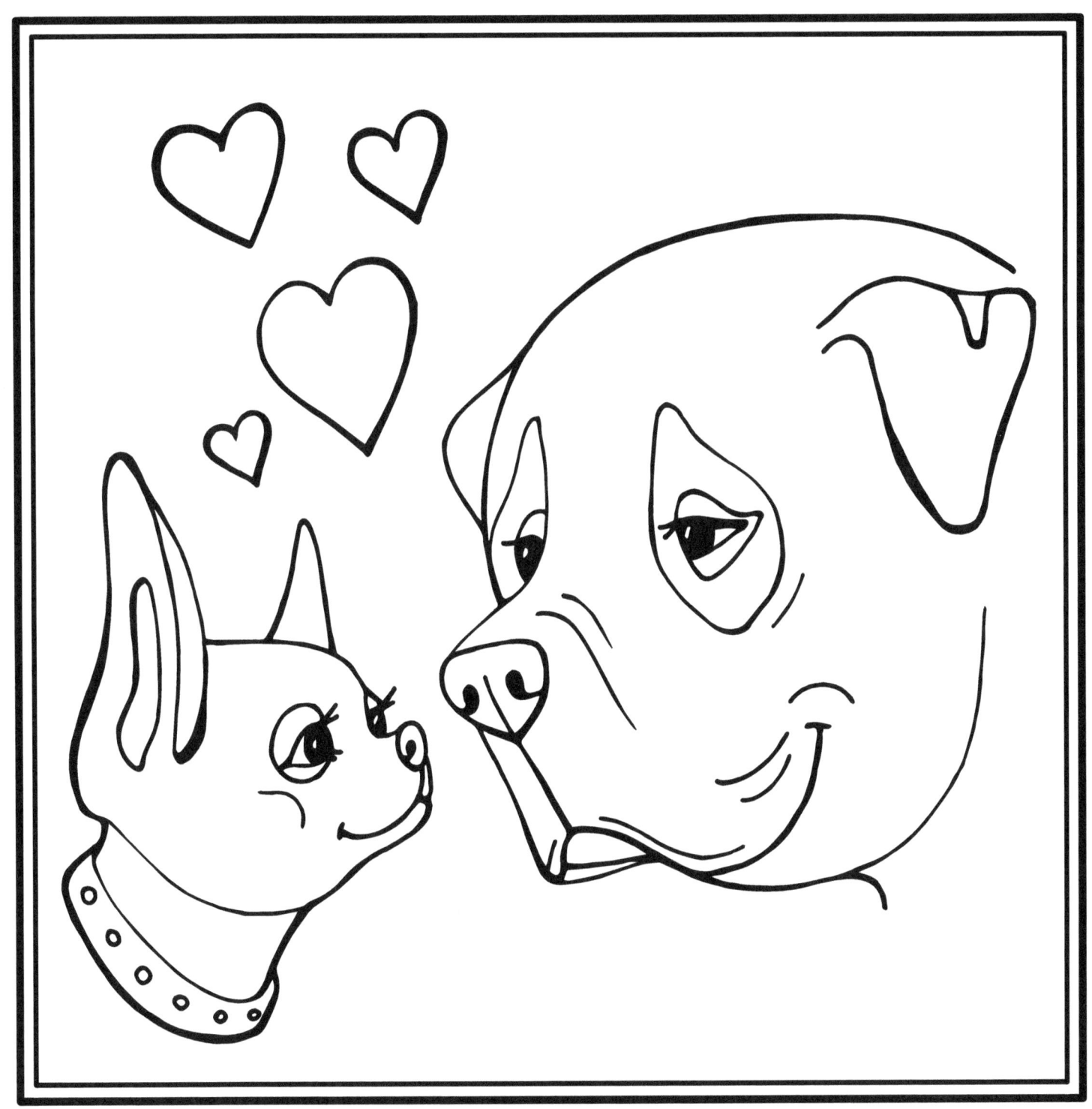

I love the Lord because he heard my plea for mercy, and listened to me.

— Psalm 116:1-2 (NET)

I will praise thee; for I am fearfully and wonderfully made: marvellous are thy works; and that my soul knoweth right well.

— Psalm 139:14 (KJV)

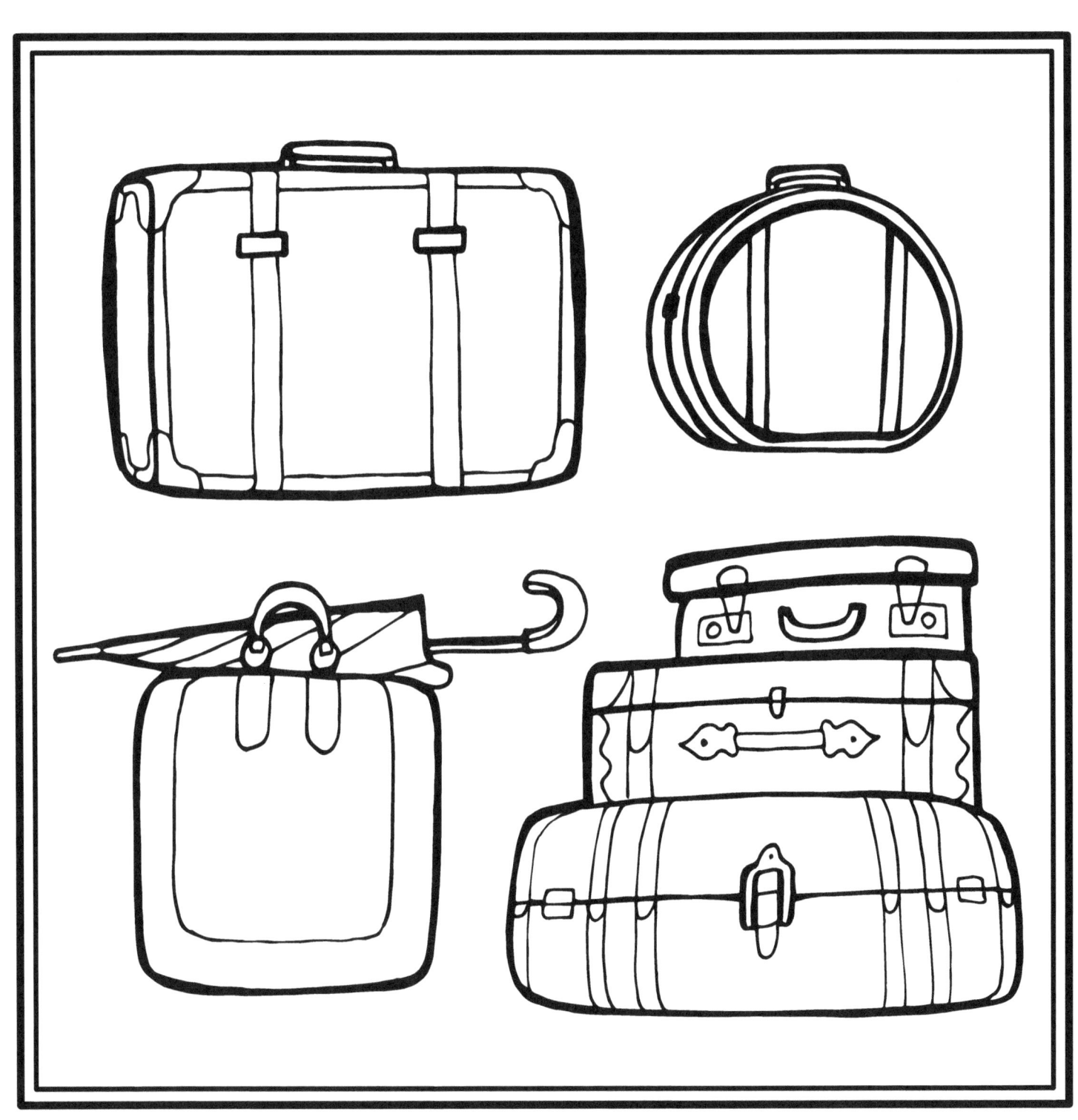

May my words and my thoughts
be acceptable in your sight, O Lord,
my sheltering rock and my redeemer.

— Psalm 19:14 (NET)

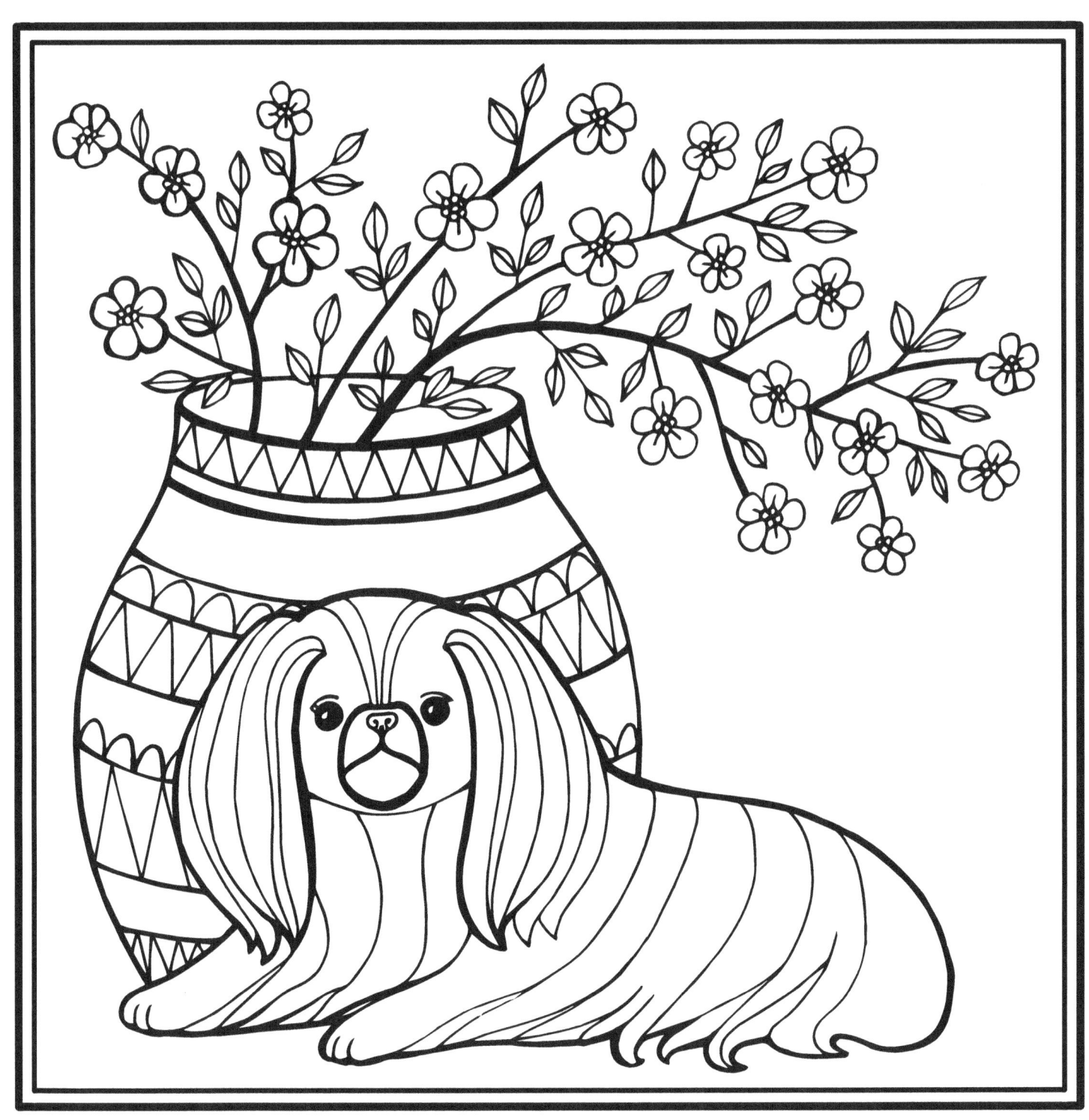

As for me, I will call upon God; and the Lord shall save me.

— Psalm 55:16 (KJV)

In the multitude of my thoughts within me thy comforts delight my soul.

— Psalm 94:19 (KJV)

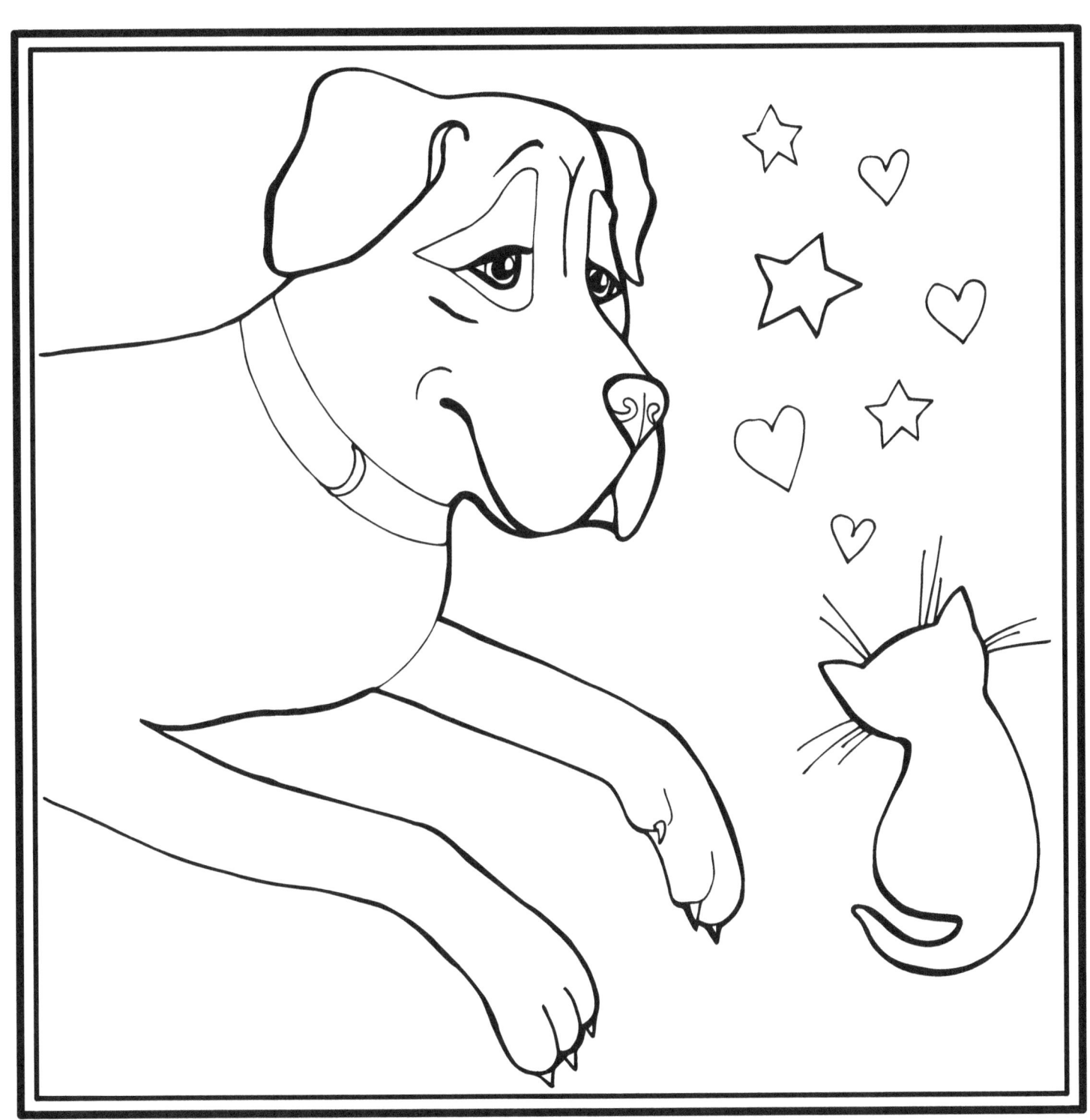

For the Lord God is a sun and shield: the Lord will give grace and glory: no good thing will he withhold from them that walk uprightly.

— Psalm 84:11 (KJV)

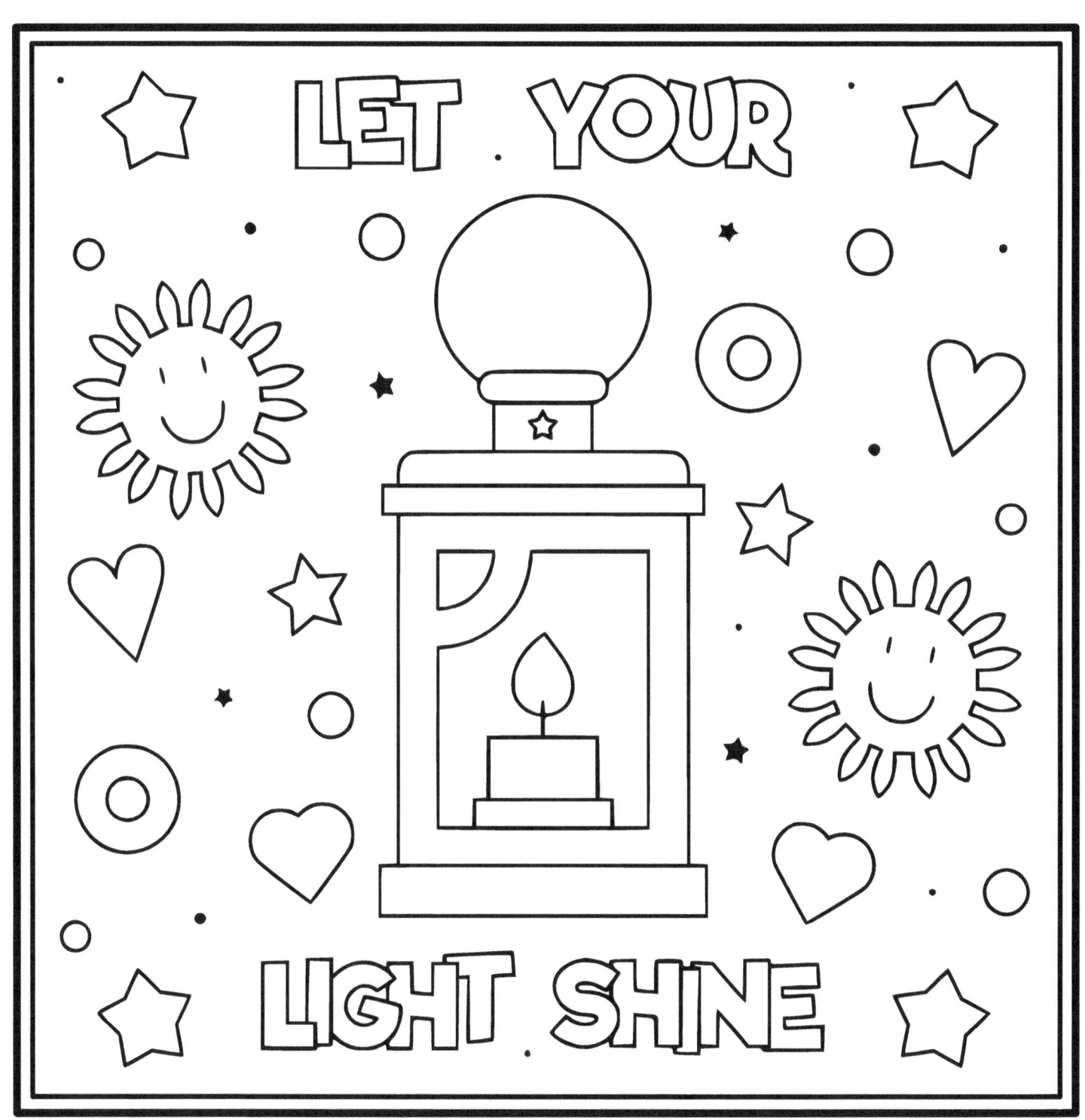

Be still, and know that I am God:
I will be exalted among the heathen,
I will be exalted in the earth.

— Psalm 46:10 (KJV)

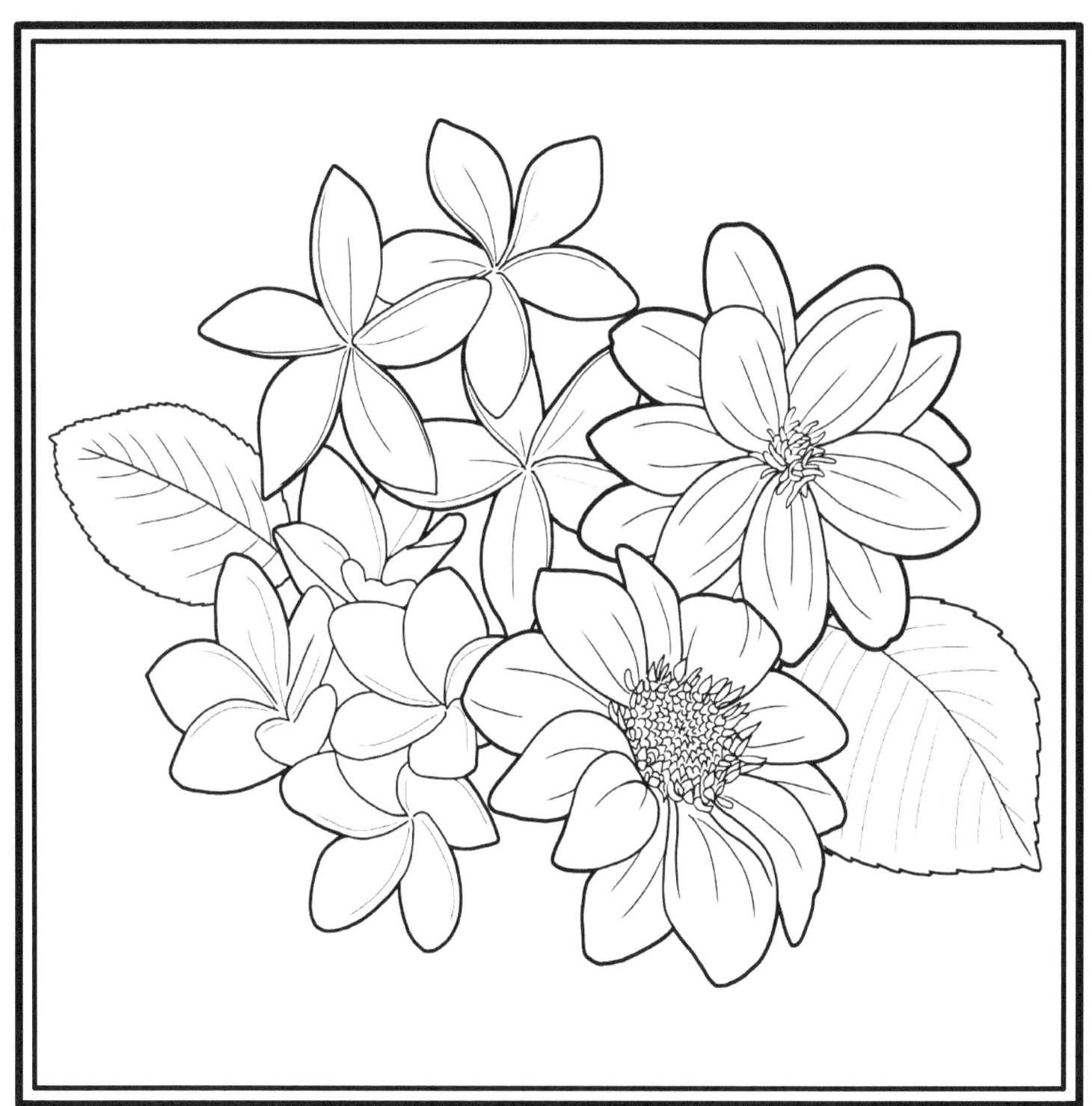

But I am continually with you; you hold my right hand. You guide me by your wise advice, and then you will lead me to a position of honor.

— Psalm 73:23-24 (NET)

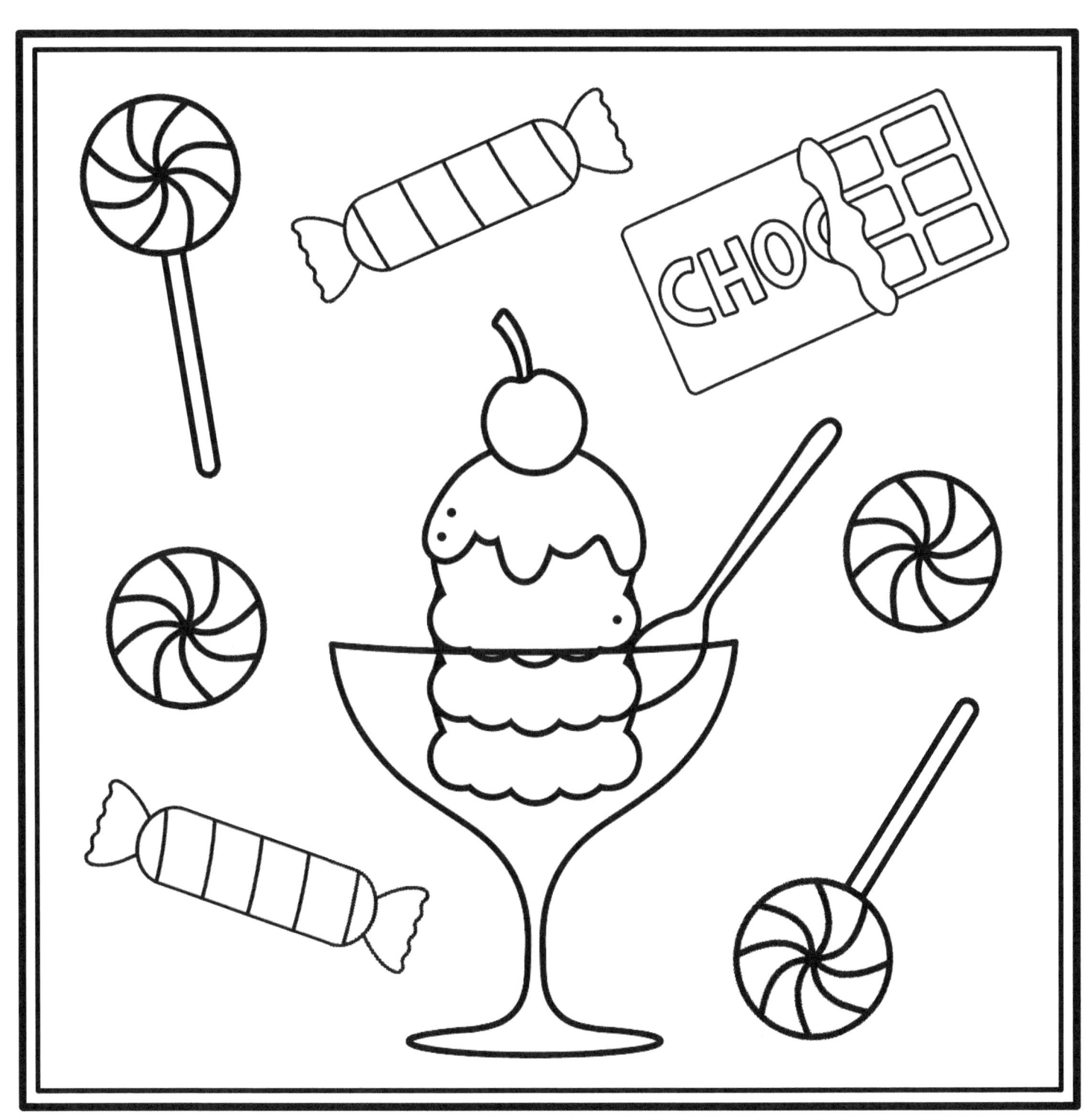

For God alone I patiently wait;
he is the one who delivers me.
He alone is my protector and deliverer.

— Psalm 62:1-2 (NET)

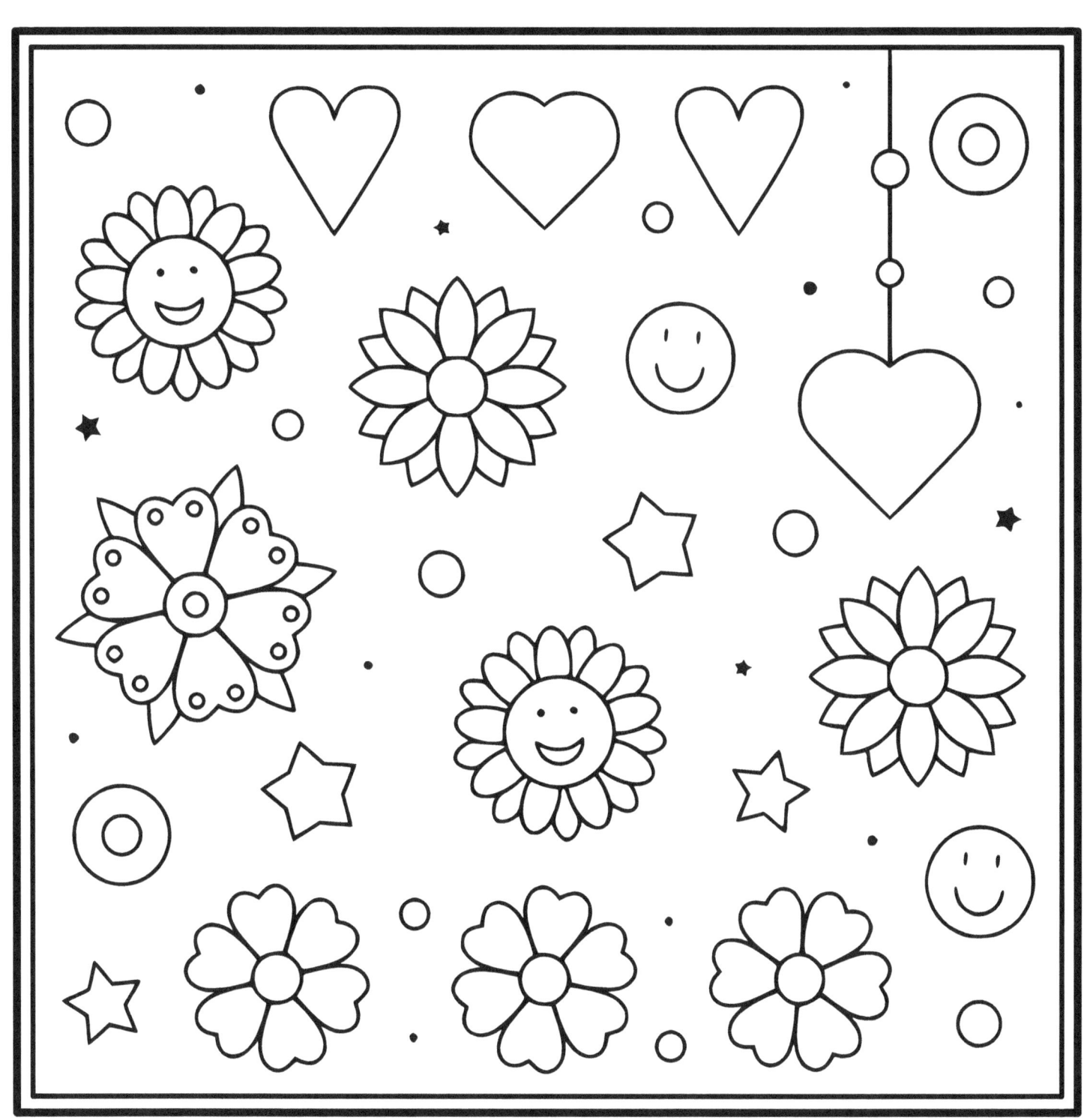

I will lie down and sleep peacefully,
for you, Lord, make me safe and secure.

— Psalm 4:8 (NET)

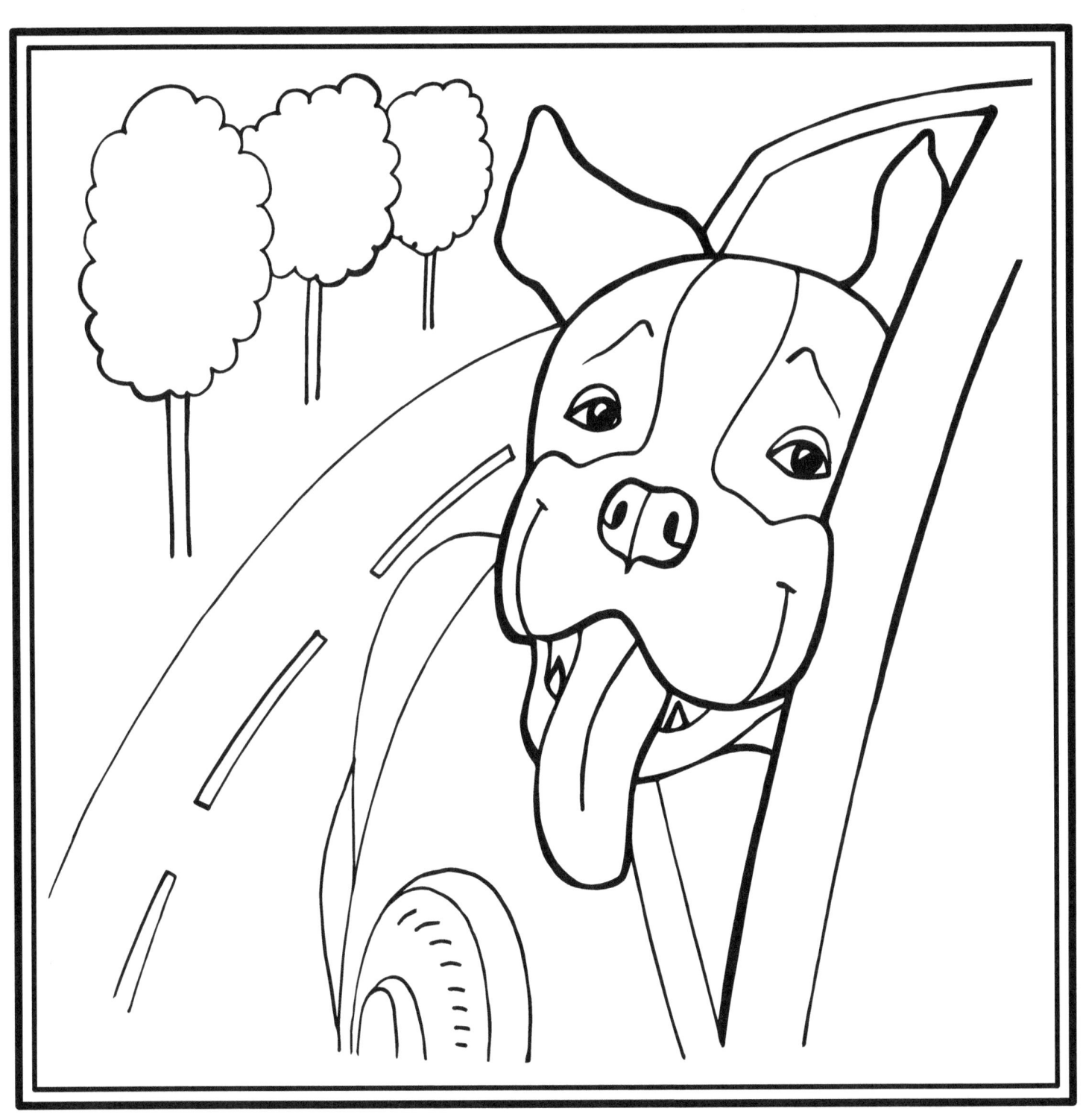

But I am continually with you; you hold my right hand. You guide me by your wise advice, and then you will lead me to a position of honor.

— Psalm 73:23-24 (NET)

Wait on the Lord: be of good courage, and he shall strengthen thine heart: wait, I say, on the Lord.

— Psalm 27:14 (KJV)

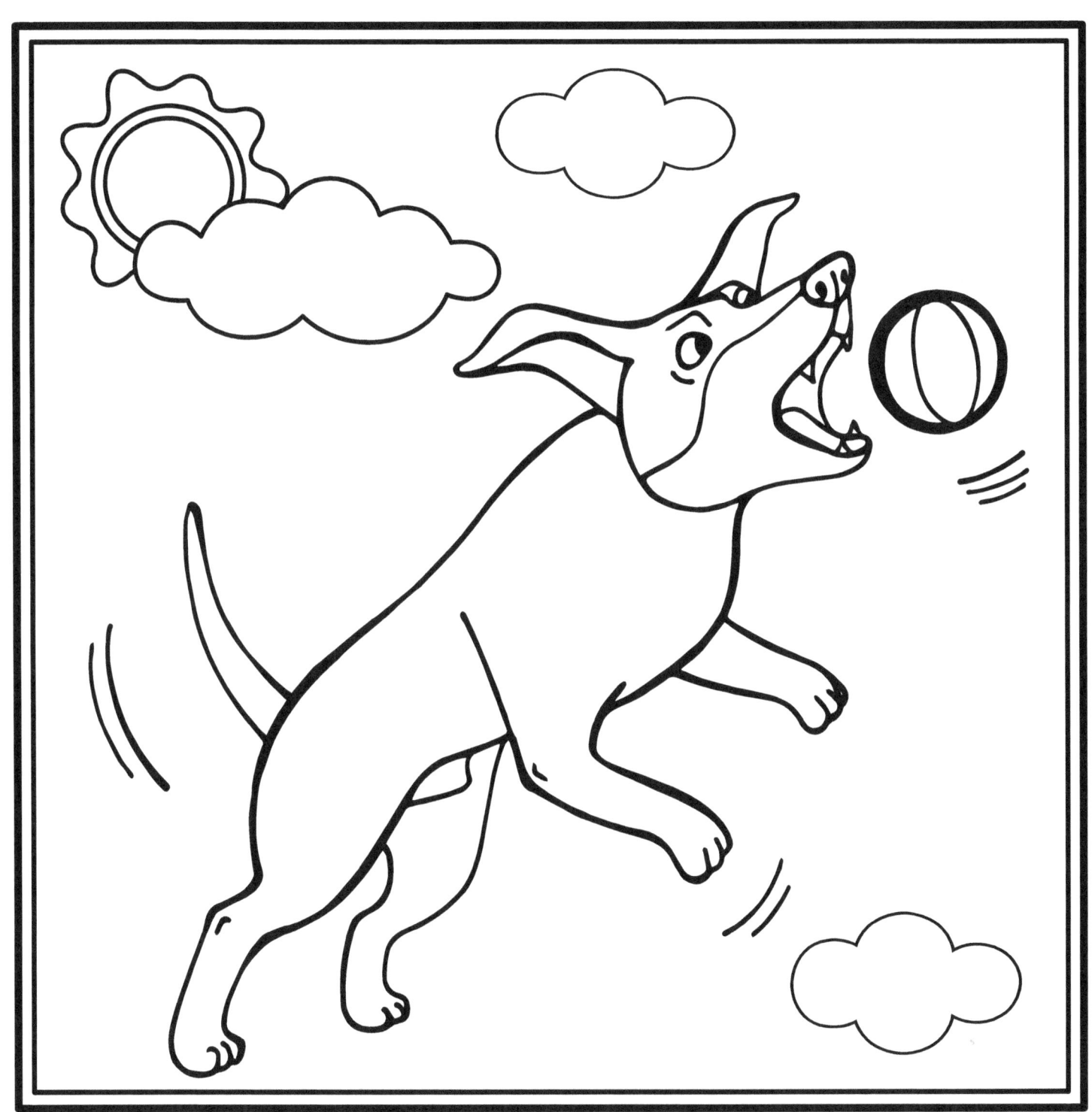

The Lord deserves praise.
Day after day he carries our burden,
the God who delivers us.

— Psalm 68:19 (NET)

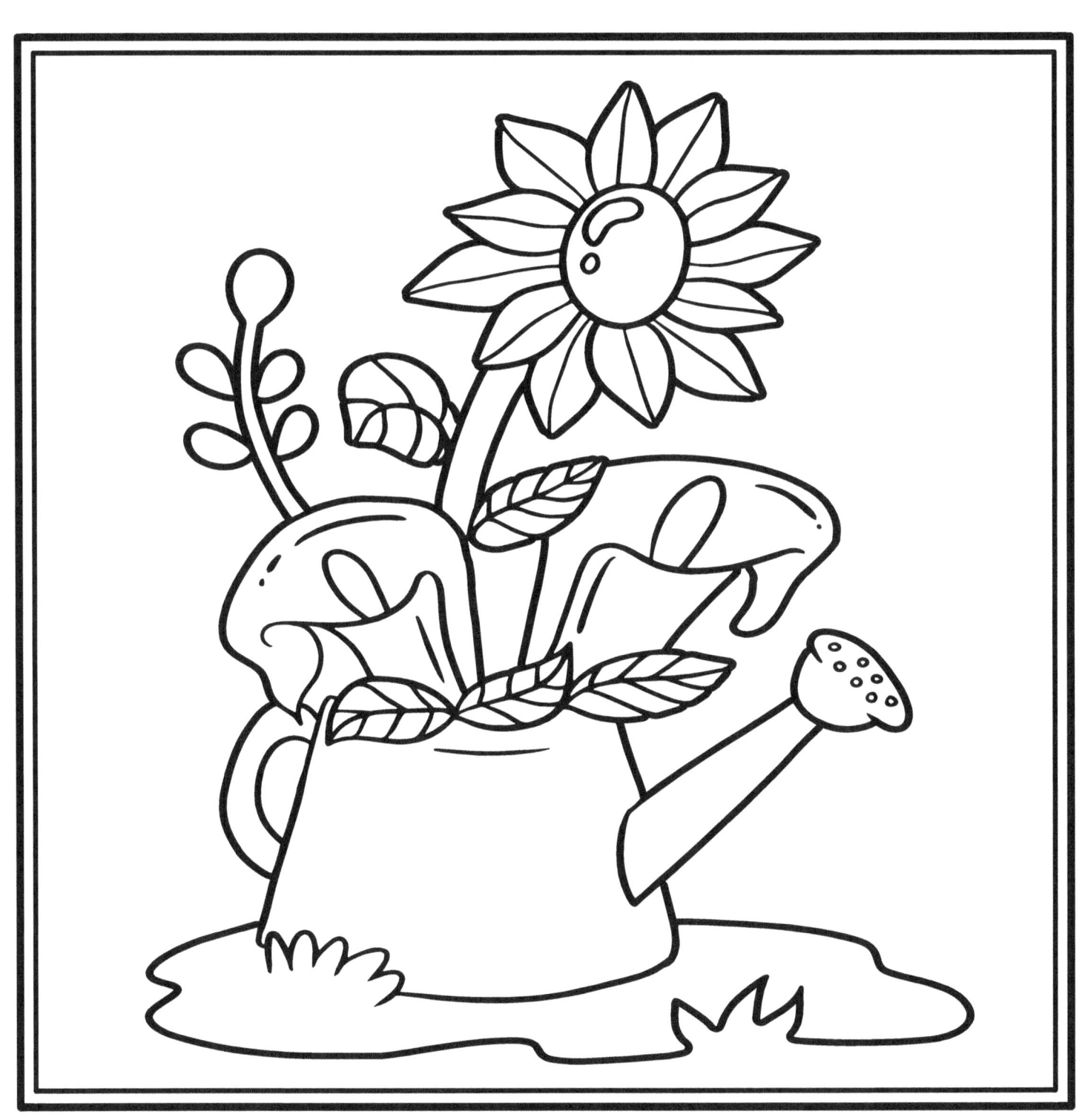

When I said, My foot slippeth; thy mercy, O Lord, held me up.

— Psalm 94:18 (KJV)

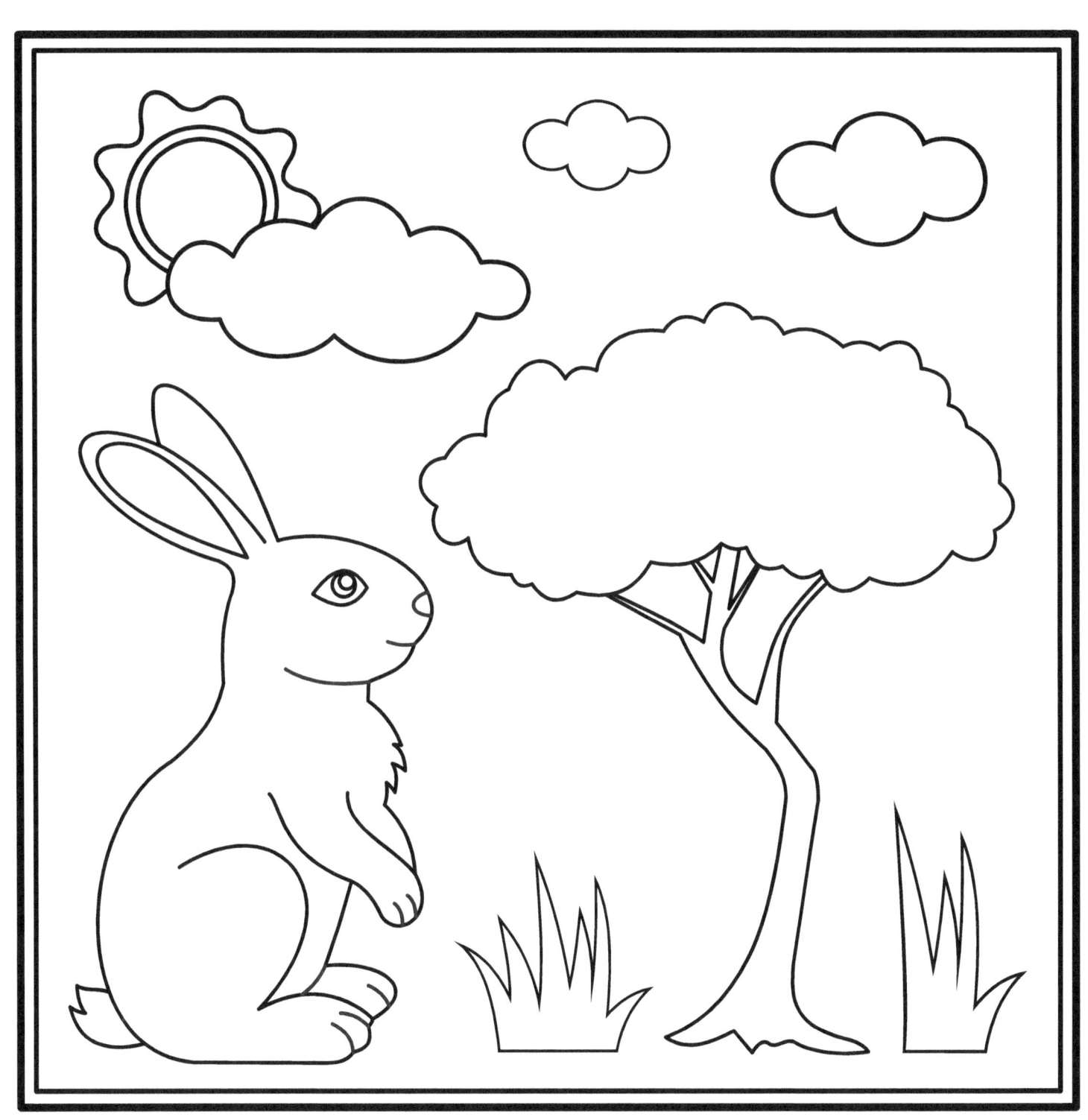

We wait for the Lord; he is our deliverer and shield. For our hearts rejoice in him, for we trust in his holy name.

— Psalm 33:20-21 (NET)

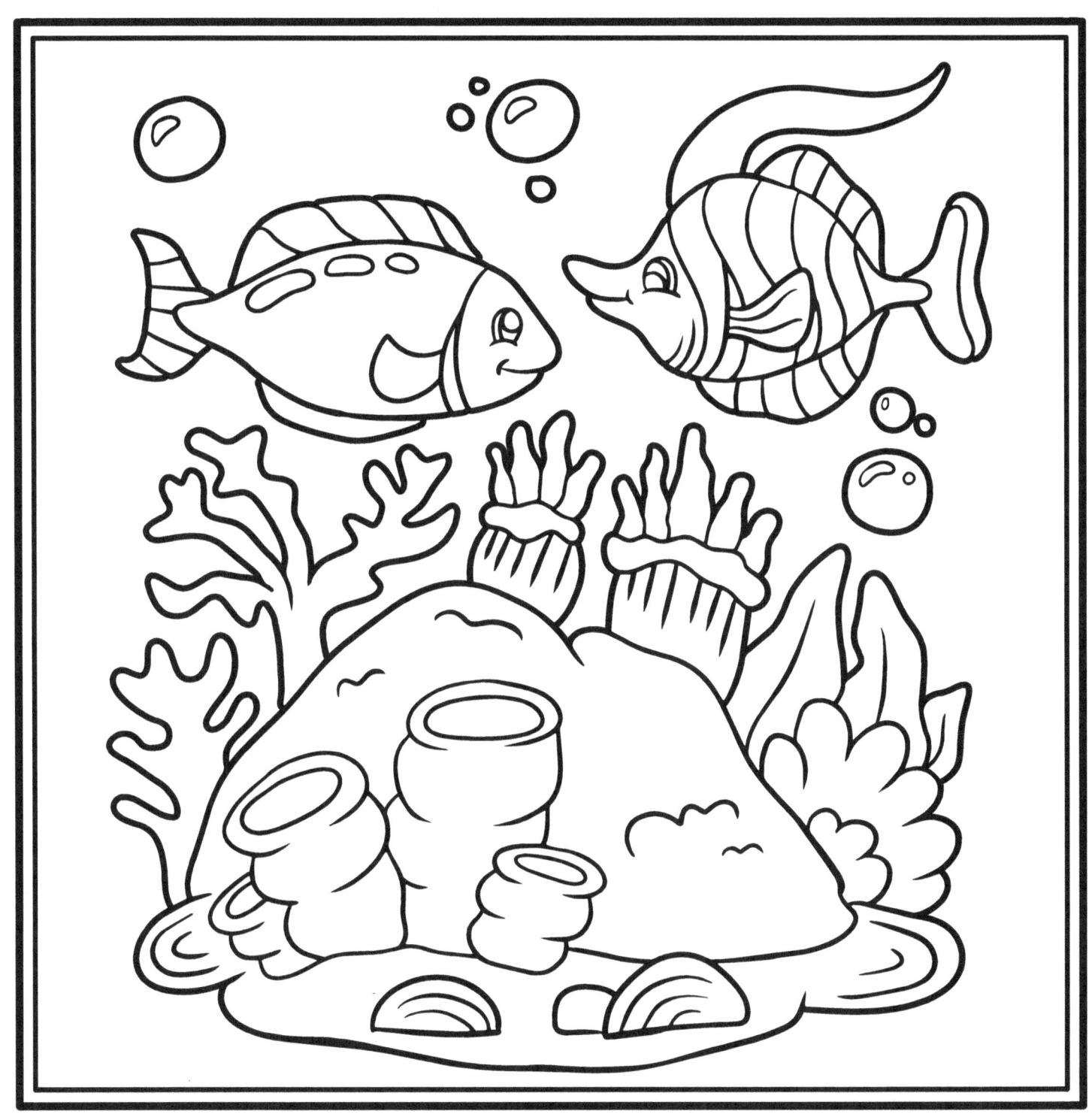

Look to him and be radiant;
do not let your faces be ashamed.

— Psalm 34:5 (NET)

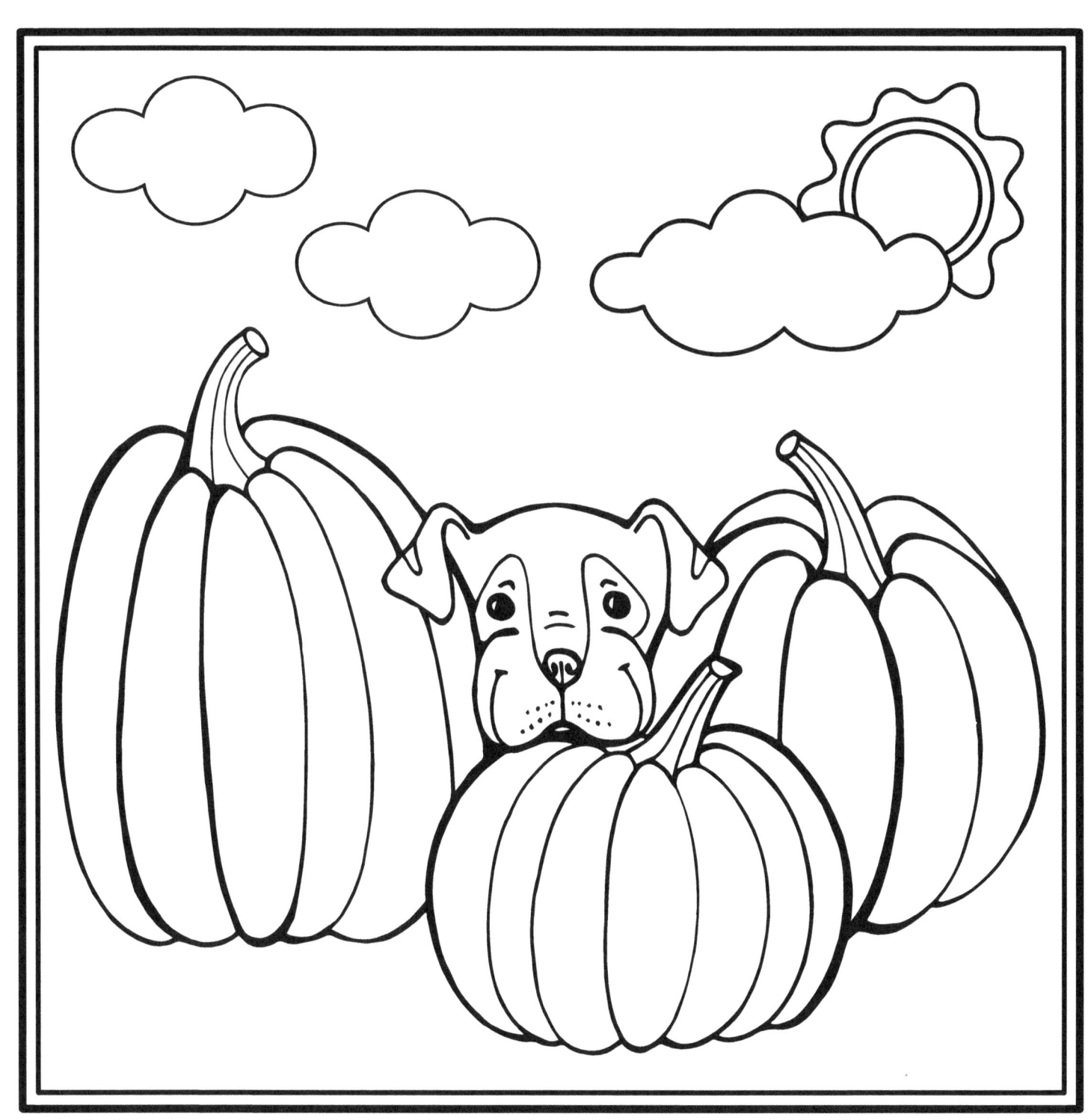

The Lord is my rock, and my fortress, and my deliverer; my God, my strength, in whom I will trust.

— Psalm 18:2 (KJV)

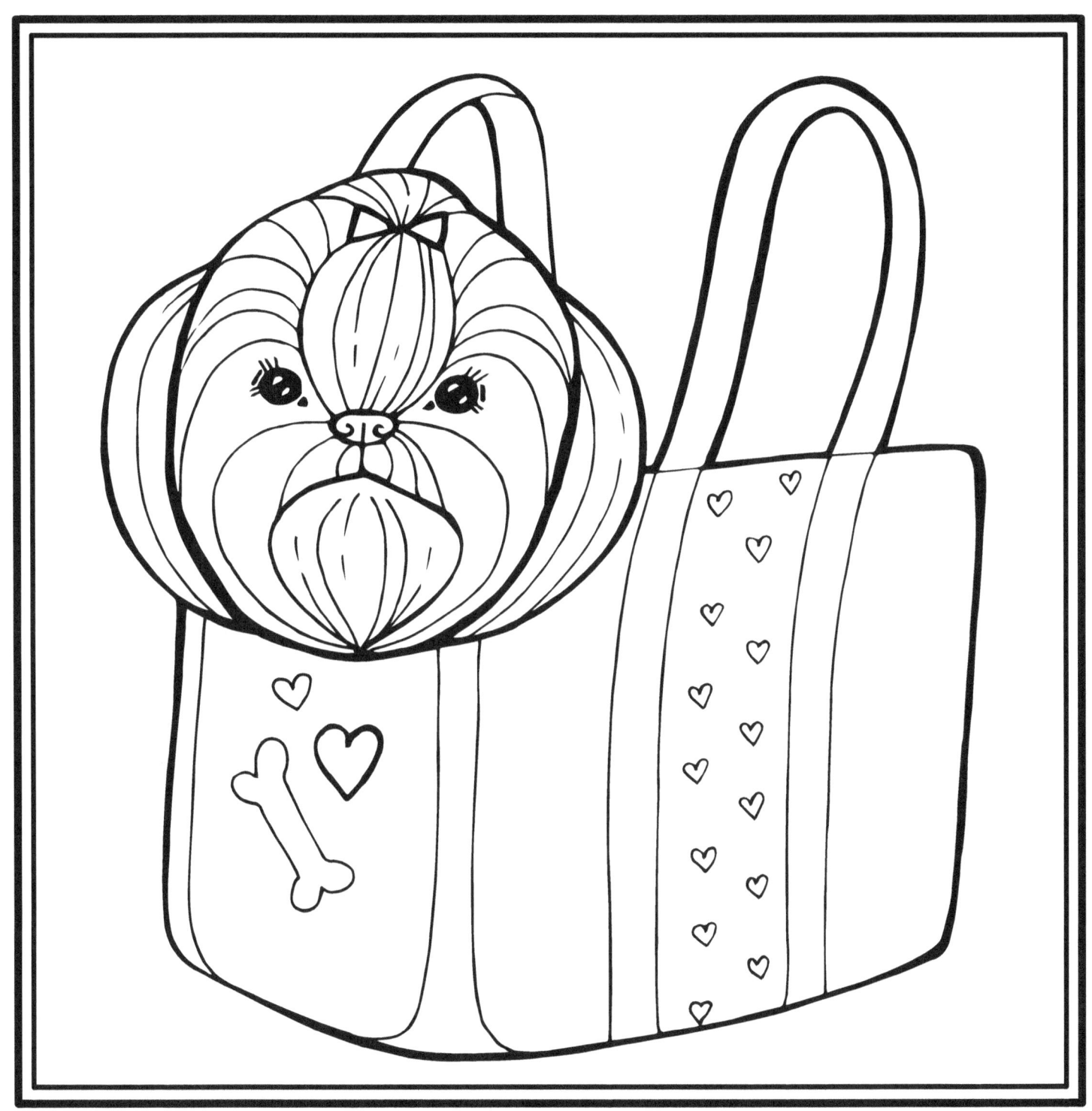

God is our strong refuge;

he is truly our helper in times of trouble.

— Psalm 46:1 (NET)

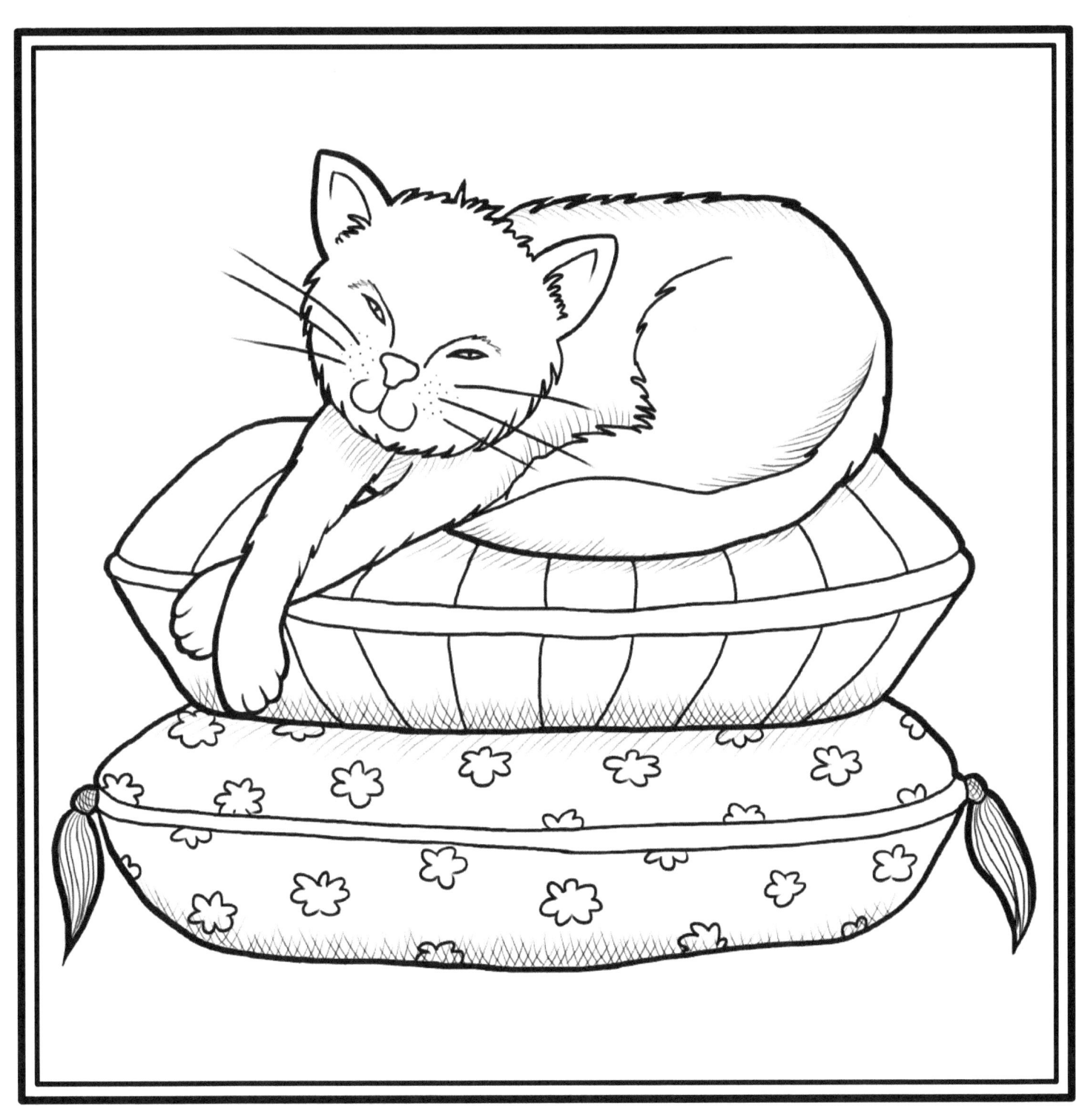

Lord, you have heard the request of the oppressed; you make them feel secure because you listen to their prayer.

— Psalm 10:17 (NET)

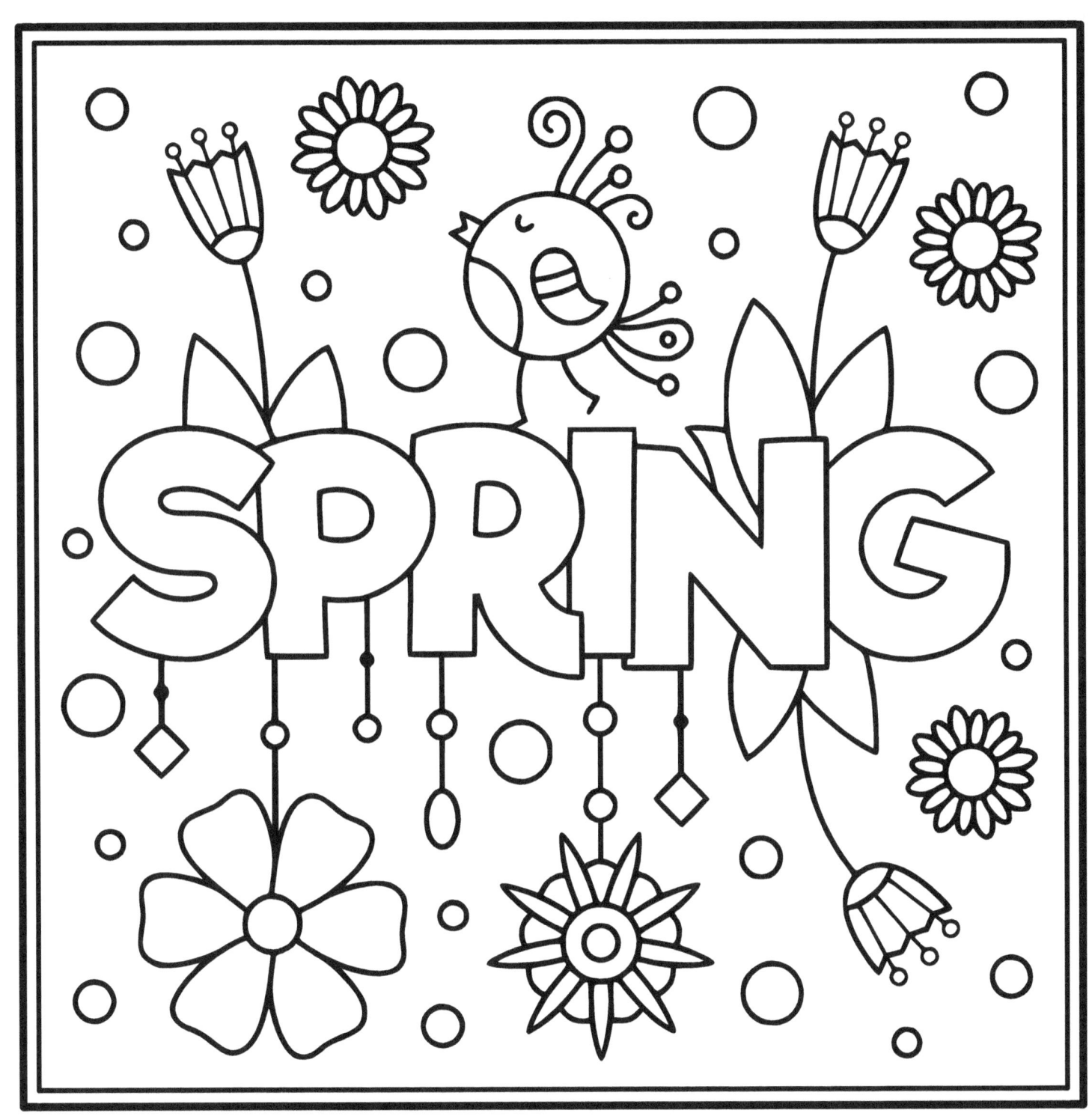

The Lord is near the brokenhearted;
he delivers those who are discouraged.

— Psalm 34:18 (NET)

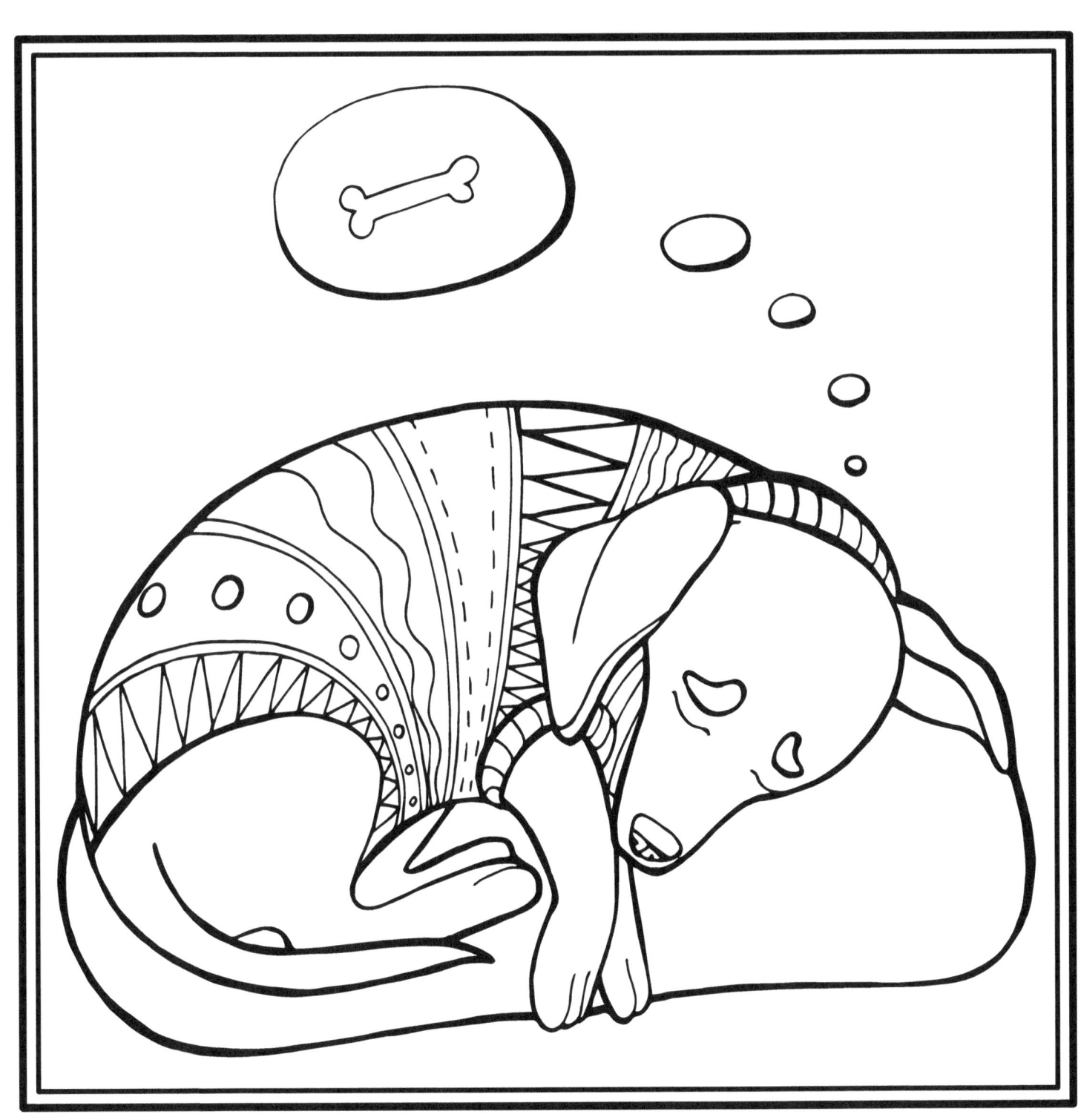

I seek your favor with all my heart.
Have mercy on me as you promised.

— Psalm 119:58 (NET)

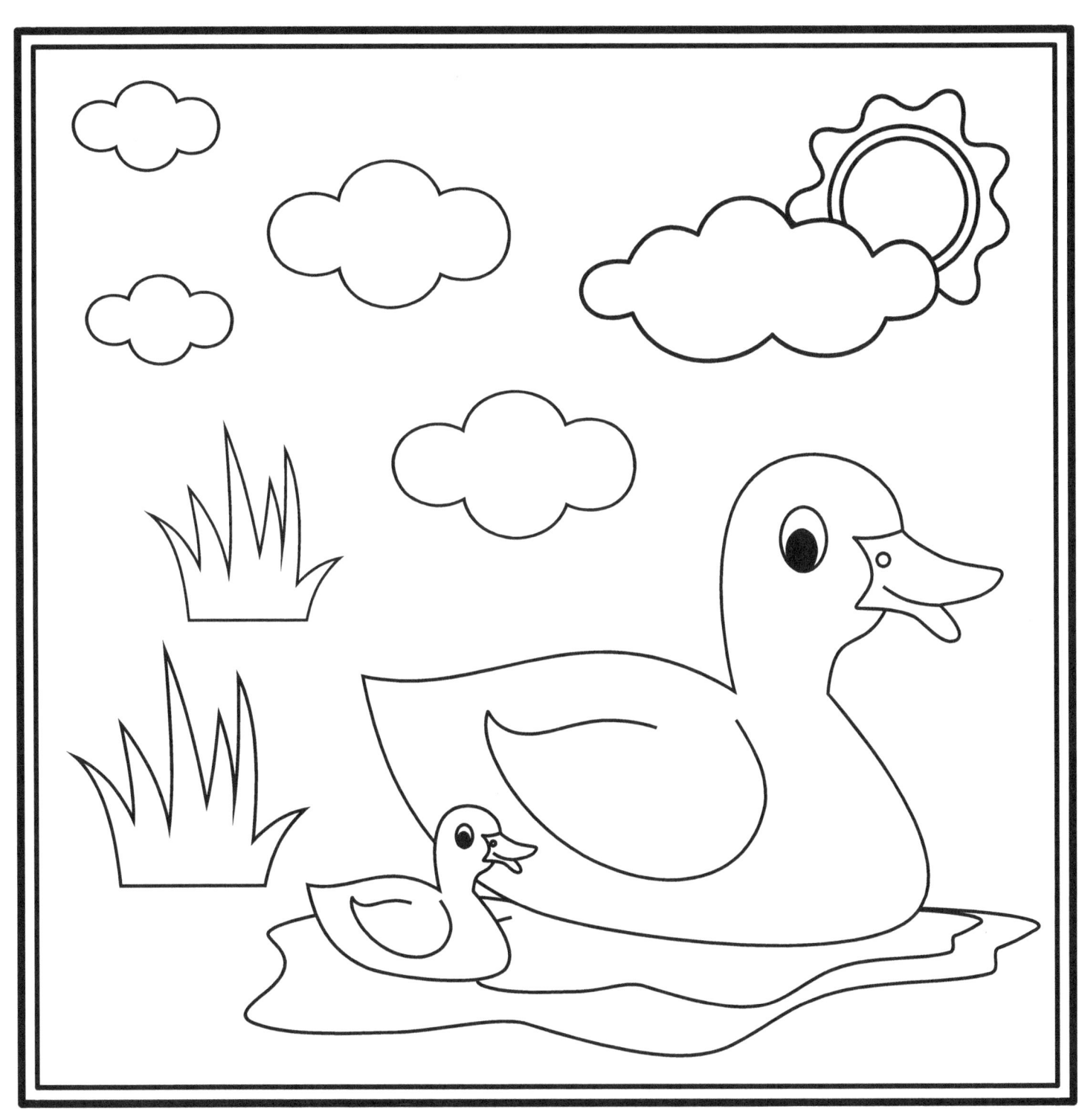

Create for me a pure heart, O God.
Renew a resolute spirit within me.

— Psalm 51:10 (NET)

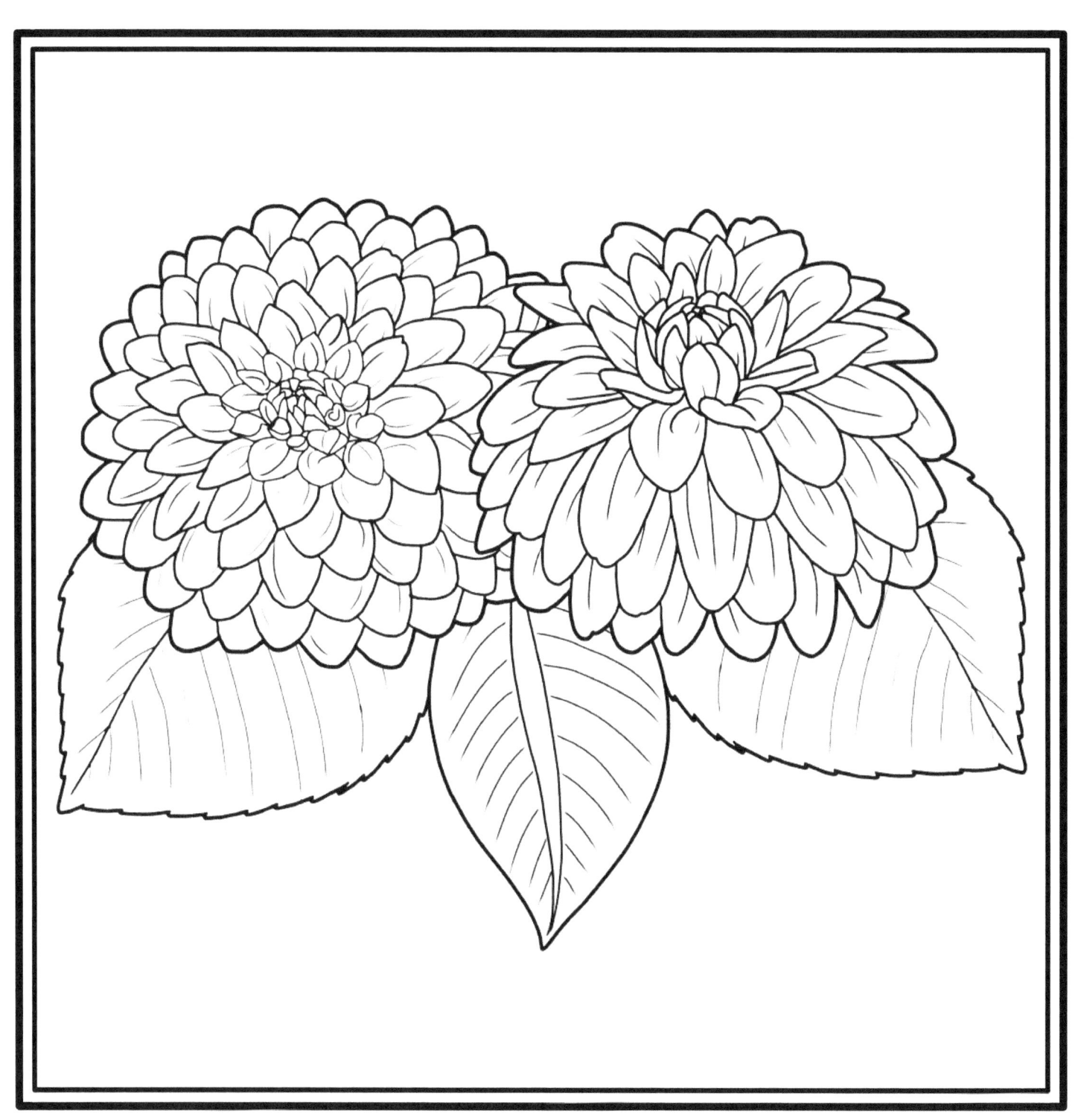

Reveal your light and your faithfulness. They will lead me; they will escort me back to your holy hill, and to the place where you live.

— Psalm 43:3 (NET)

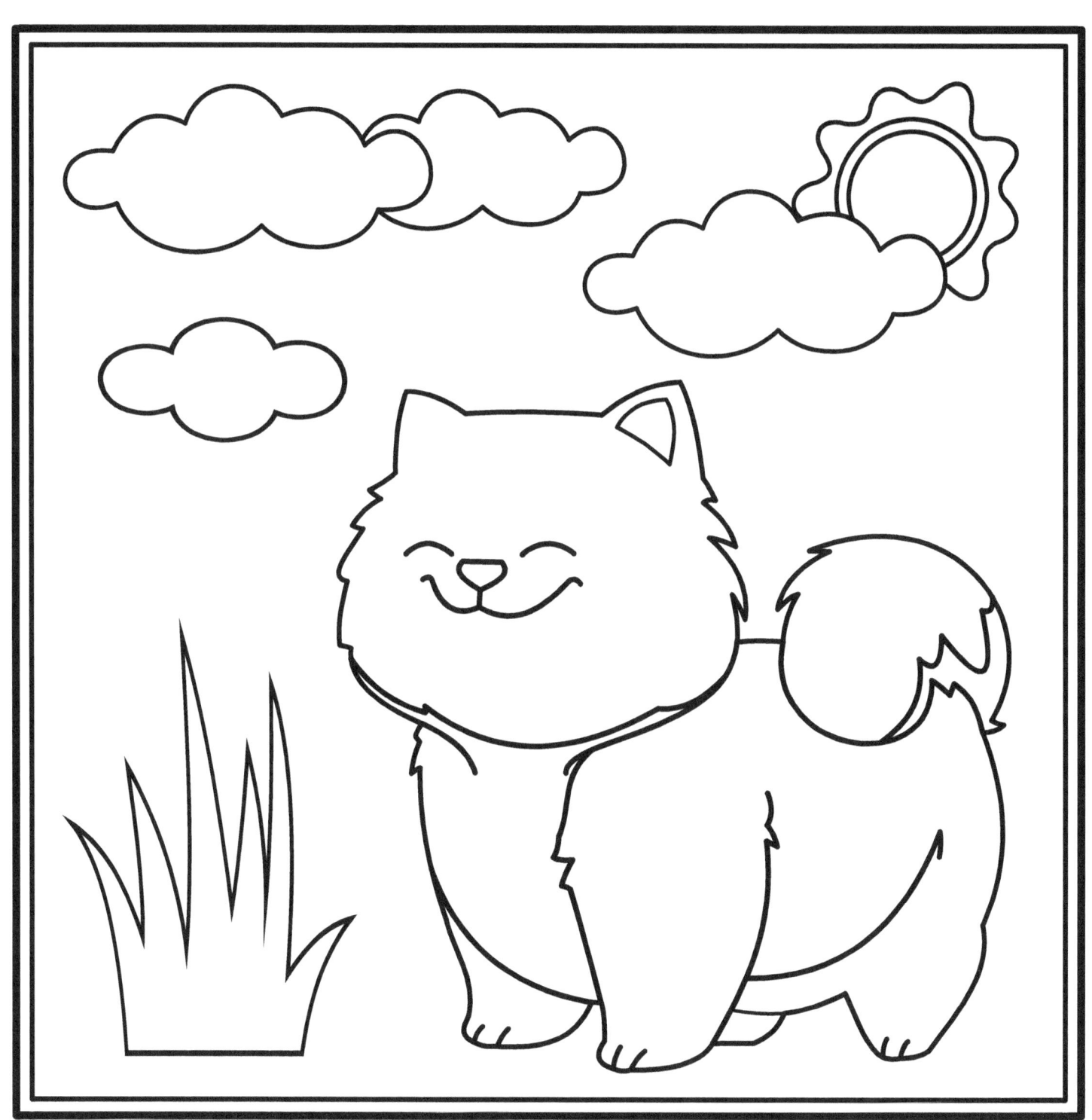

You lead me in the path of life.
I experience absolute joy in your presence;
you always give me sheer delight.

— Psalm 16:11 (NET)

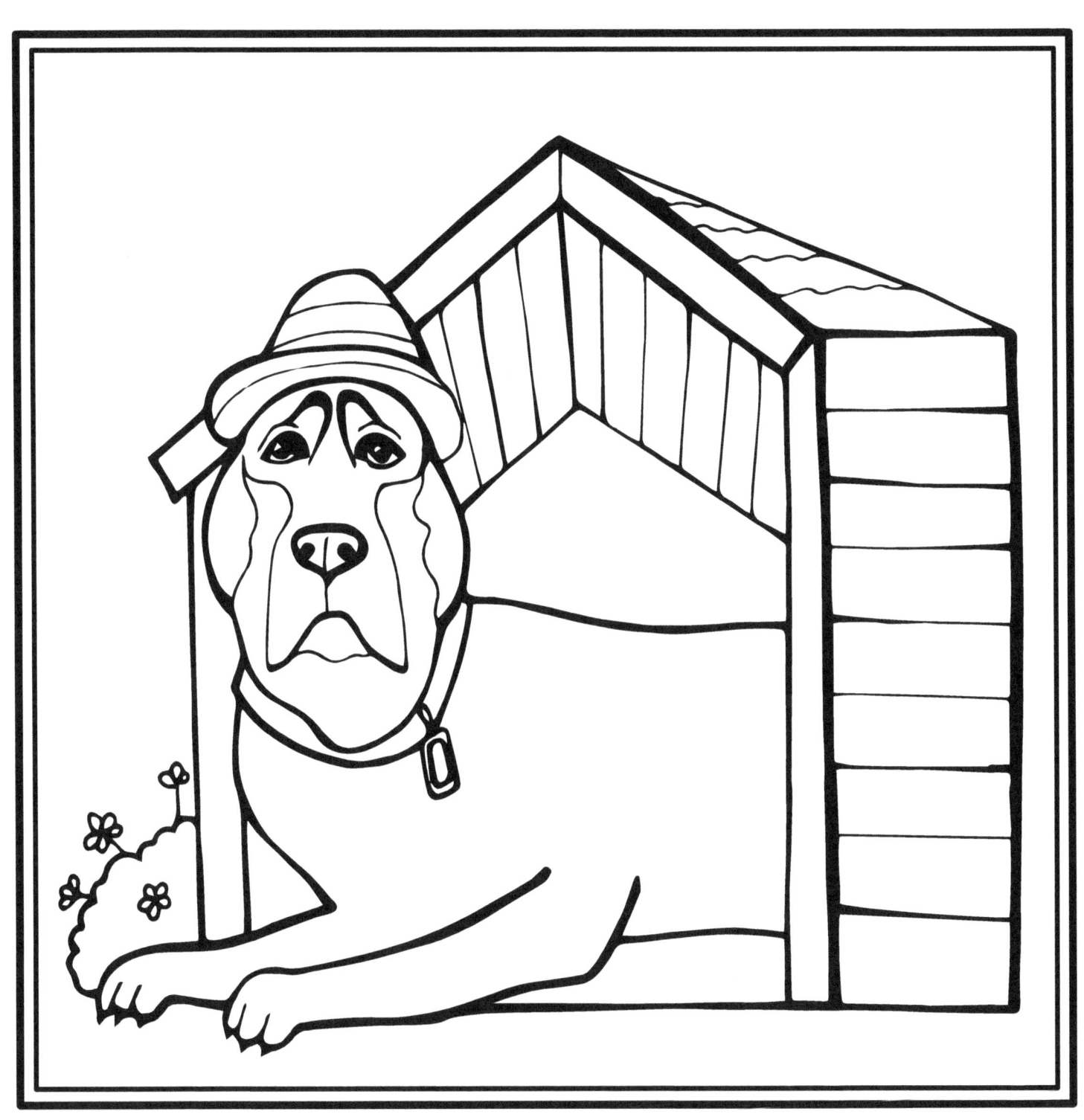

I sought the Lord's help and he answered me;
he delivered me from all my fears.

— Psalm 34:4 (NET)

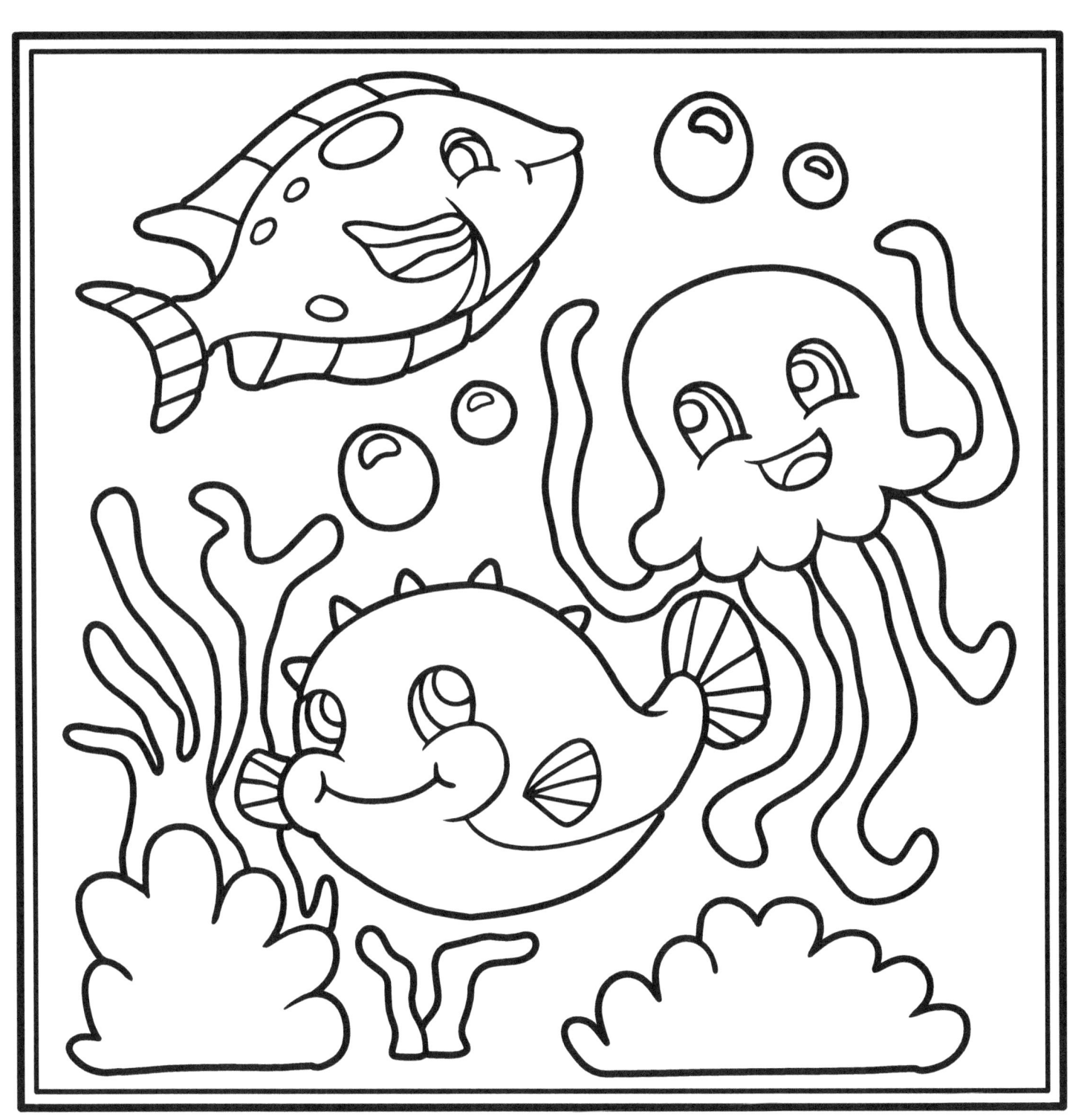

Take delight in the Lord, and he will answer your prayers.

— Psalm 37:4 (NET)

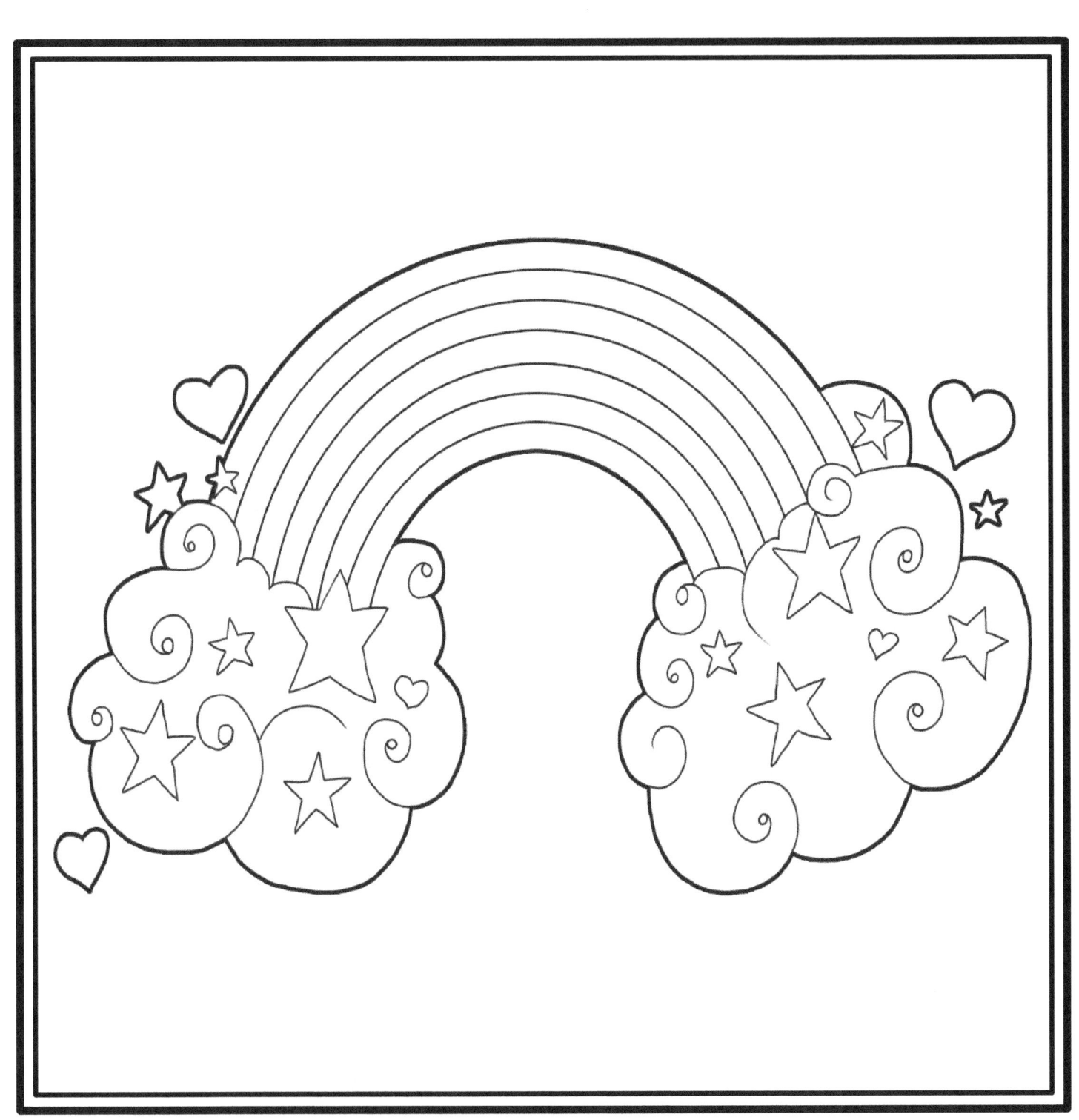

Thy word is a lamp unto my feet,
and a light unto my path.

— Psalm 119:105 (KJV)

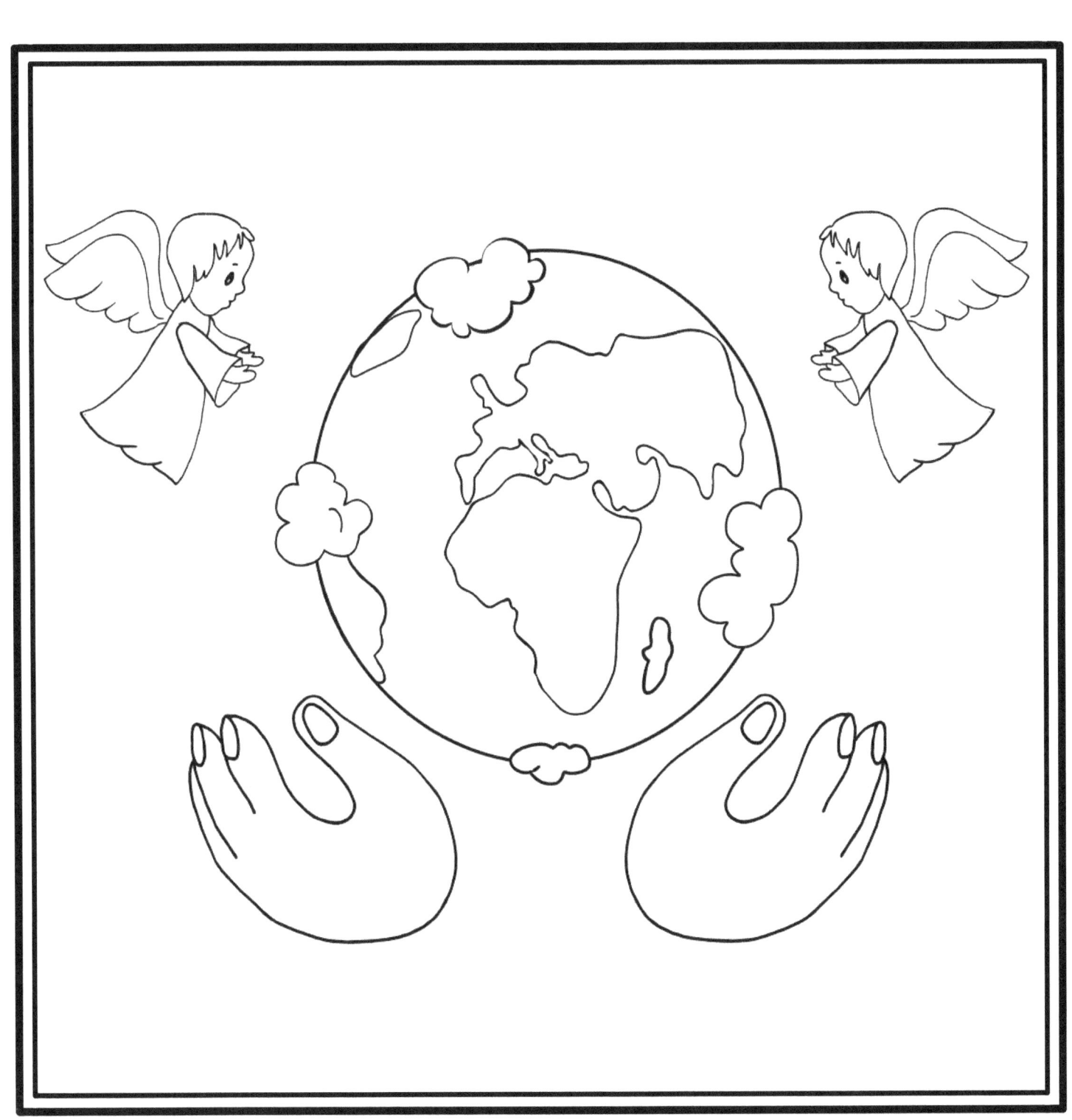

The Lord is near all who cry out to him,
all who cry out to him sincerely.

— Psalm 145:18 (NET)

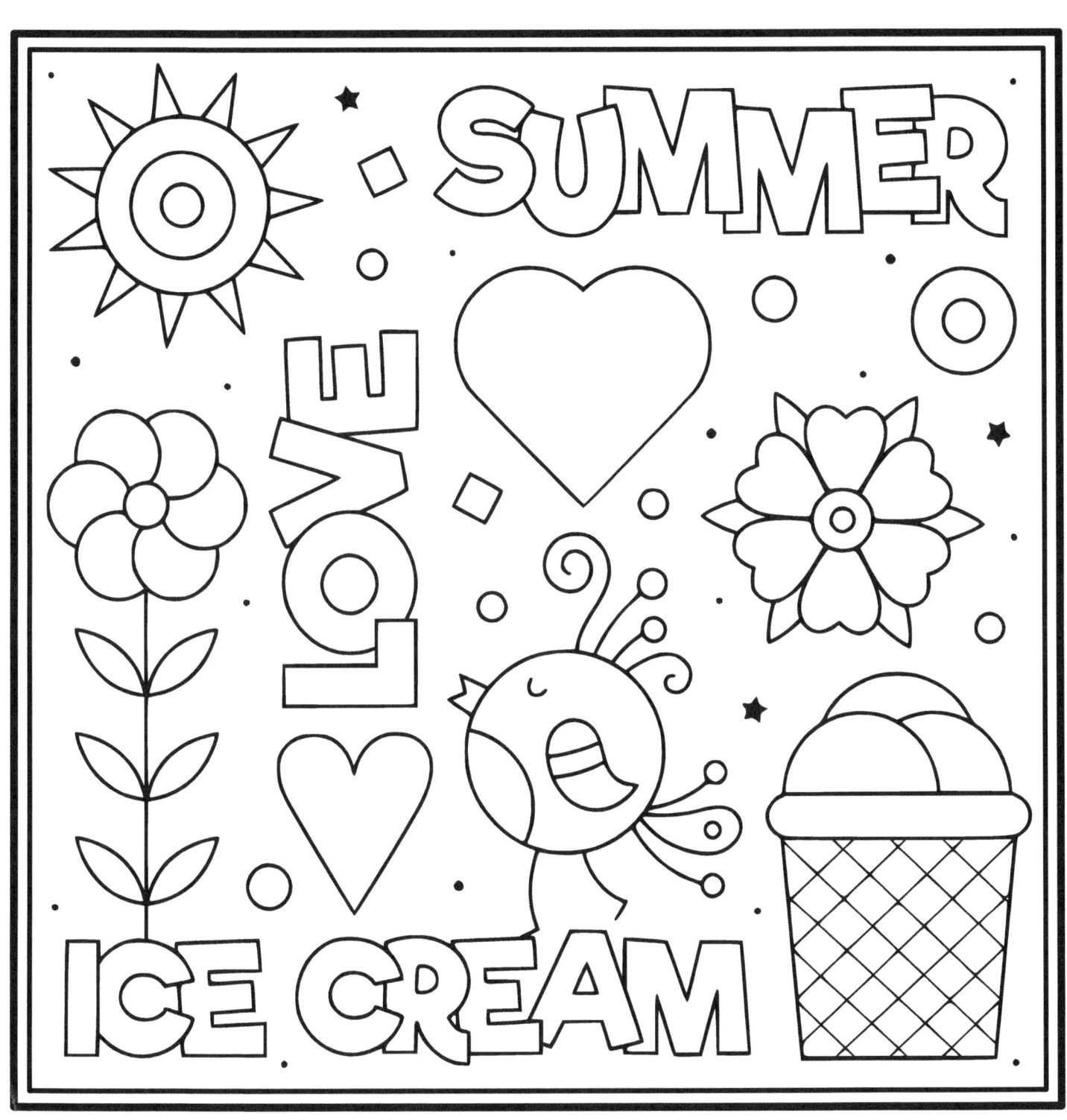

He will shelter you with his wings;
you will find safety under his wings.
His faithfulness is like a shield.

— Psalm 91:4 (NET)

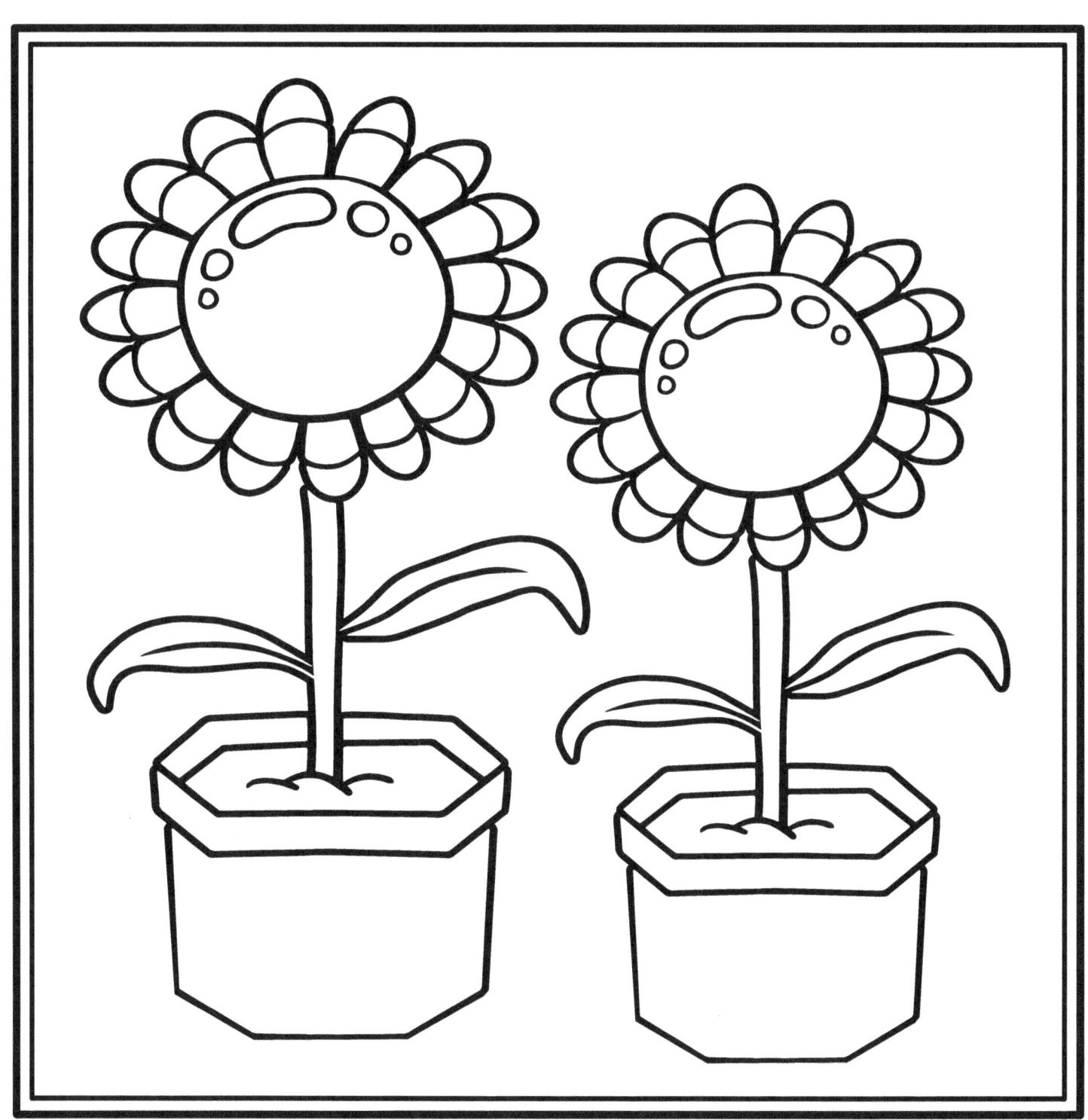

www.ingramcontent.com/pod-product-compliance
Lightning Source LLC
Chambersburg PA
CBHW080514220526
45465CB00006B/2479